THE WINE BIBBER'S BIBLE

a practical guide to selecting and enjoying wines

THE WINE BIBBER'S BIBLE

Second Revised Version

BY JAMES NORWOOD PRATT

with the collaboration of
JACQUES de CASO

drawings by
SARA RAFFETTO

published by
101 PRODUCTIONS
San Francisco

ACKNOWLEDGEMENTS

Excerpts have been quoted from
the following books with the
generous permission of their publishers.

Hilaire Belloc. *Advice.*
Harvill Press, London.
Copyright © 1960 Bridget Grant.

Creighton Churchill. *The World of Wines.*
The Macmillan Company, New York.
Copyright © 1963, 1964 Creighton Churchill.

Hugh Johnson. *Wine.*
Simon and Schuster, New York;
Thomas Nelson and Sons, London.
Copyright © 1966 Hugh Johnson.

Illuminated initials designed and executed by
John Immel.
Maps designed and executed by John C.W. Carroll.

Copyright © 1971, 1975 James Norwood Pratt
Copyright © 1981 Spagyric Arts, Inc.
Illustrations © 1971, 1975, 1981 Sara Raffetto

John Melville, *Guide to California Wines.*
Nourse Publishing, San Carlos.
Third Edition, revised by Jefferson Morgan;
Copyright © 1968 Jefferson Morgan.

George Saintsbury. *Notes on a Cellarbook.*
St. Martin's Press, New York;
The Macmillan Company of Canada;
The Macmillan Company of London.
Copyright © 1933 The Macmillan Company.

Allan Sichel et al. *A Guide to Good Wine.*
Copyright © 1970 Murrays Sales and
Service Company, Publishers, London.

With especial acknowledgements to
colleagues Brian St. Pierre,
Dominick Cagliostro and Jim Lucas.

Library of Congress Cataloging in Publication Data

Pratt, James Norwood.
   The wine bibber's bible.

   Includes index.

   1. Wine and wine making.   I. De Caso, Jacques,
1928-   joint author.   II. Title.
TP548.P737   1981   641.2'22   80-24680
ISBN   0-89286-182-7

Printed in the United States of America.
All rights reserved.
Distributed to the book trade in the United States by
Charles Scribner's Sons, New York

Published by
101 PRODUCTIONS,
834 Mission Street, San Francisco, California 94103

CONTENTS

TO JOHN, SUSAN, ROSALYN, GETTYS, BLISS & CHARLOT
Do what thou wilt shall be the whole of the Law

'Twas honest old Noah first planted the vine
And mended his morals by drinking its wine
He justly the drinking of water decried
For he knew that all Mankind by drinking it died.

From this Piece of History plainly we find
That Water's good neither for Body or Mind;
That Virtue and Safety in Wine-bibbing's found
While all that drink water deserve to be drowned.

—from an Ergo Bibamus by B. Franklin, 1745

Thirst is wine's sole reason for existence—simple thirst. Wine is a sure cure for present thirst and an excellent preventive against the thirst to come. As much admitted, what makes wine subject to bookwriting when several species of bedbug are still unclassified—what? The Label. The label is the last and most terrible test a wine must pass before its thirst-quenchability gets to speak for itself. Consider the wines called Californian. You might have considered them sooner were they not so called. They are nevertheless as serviceable as any for purposes of addiction, pride of possession and pretentiousness—in which respect they are, now, like all other wines. Though remaining differences between Californian and other wines may appear small, all differences are small and small differences are decisive. Californian wines are not as yet classified, codified and variously guaranteed as European wines have been. No long-standing authority has eliminated discovery and surprises from the drinking of them. That's what makes a book like this possible—but not what makes *them* unique. This is simply what the grape says in California which it pronounces nowhere else.

All wines may have the same food value, but their spiritual or soul food value varies enormously. A famous composer used to prescribe Champagne for himself when he was working on comic opera, Rhine wine for religious music and Burgundy when his theme was heroic. Wine drinking, properly understood, is a mystical operation. Man in his natural state and wine combine like the Father and the Son in the Trinity to engender a Holy Spirit, a superior man, an exalted and expanded state of being. To judge the spiritual and aesthetic properties of Californian wines in terms of European is as technically correct and as completely misleading as to call Lot the patriarch one of the Sodomites.

Peering into the darkness of a wine critic's mind is safest with glass in hand, as the blaze of enophiliac fervor about to commence should prove. It is written out of the strangest of all the strange things that move within us, the mysterious preference for the best—and also in hope of royalty enough to afford it.

James Norwood Pratt
San Francisco

WINE WRIT
Any last words?

Thank you California for your wine
Thank you for your sweet and bitter fruit.

—*The Rolling Stones*

merica's first wine was a 1564 vintage made by Spaniards from grapes that were growing wild in Florida. From the very first days of colonization the Spaniards took the grapevine with them everywhere they went in the New World. Cortés himself established this grape growing policy in Mexico, primarily to insure that there would always be wine enough for the mass to be celebrated. Thus when Father Junipero Serra in 1769 founded at San Diego the first of the missions he was to establish in California, obedient to Spain's policy and mindful of the church's needs, he planted California's first grapevines there. The "Mission" grape is still grown in California and probably today produces no worse wine than it did back then. Those early Spanish had probably found this variety growing in Sardinia (where it grows to this day), and chose it because it was easily transplanted and hardy enough to survive anywhere. And survive it did, at all twenty-one of the missions where it was planted, being made into both wine of a sort and brandy, as the old mission records show: "Father Duran at Santa Barbara made *aguardiente* as clear as crystal, or when treated with burnt sugar, of a clear yellow. It was doubly distilled and as strong as the reverend father's faith."

Catholic grape

In 1823, the year the last of the missions was founded in Sonoma, Joseph Chapman in Los Angeles became the first Californian to seek a livelihood raising grapes and selling wine. Chapman, Yankee and entrepreneur and a one-time pirate, soon had a competitor in the person of Jean-Louis Vignes, a cooper from Bordeaux who brought with him the first French vines to grace the soil of California. The appropriately named Vignes established El Aliso, his ranch and vineyard, in the heart of present-day Los

commercial growers

Angeles; by 1840 he was able to ship quantities of dry white wine and of *aguardiente* to San Francisco. (And at outrageous prices: two dollars and four dollars the gallon, respectively.)

"... and in 1841 appeared Benjamin Davis Wilson, a Southerner in a fringed jacket, who instantly took to the milieu, planted his acres, and became Don Benito, one with the grandees. The transplantation was a happy one; he throve like the indigenous toyon-bush, became more Spaniard than the natives, grew fair wine, less good than Don Luis Vignes' Claret, bought ranch after ranch, and hacked a road up a mountain that he admired, and a convenience it was for the astronomers who later built their Mt. Wilson telescope upon it. His land was Oak Knoll, the site now of the Huntington Library at San Marino. Don Benito became the first mayor of Los Angeles, and the last, they say, to know the grape, and on pouring a bottle to utter in the Spanish way a prayer to the vine-dressers whose care made it a wine worth pouring."

a Southerner

So runs the account given by Idwal Jones, stylist *extraordinaire,* and it is to his *Vines in the Sun* you must turn for a complete (and completely entertaining) history of the wines and vines of California before 1900. But not even so short a synopsis of that fascinating history as this one can dismiss in a few lines the career of Agoston Haraszthy, visionary and adventurer. Should you wonder how a Hungarian nobleman came to be devoured by alligators in Nicaragua in 1869, you will allow us a digression long enough to tell his story.

Agoston Haraszthy

Haraszthy had given up his hereditary title of count for the more democratic one of colonel before he set out for California at the head of a wagon train in 1849. His destination, however, was not the gold fields of the north but rather San Diego where he thought to find the best land for winegrowing. Vineyards had kept the Haraszthys wealthy for centuries in Hungary, but Agoston had been forced to flee his native soil when the popular uprising in which he played a role had collapsed and the reactionary government placed a price on his head. With characteristic decisiveness he straightway betook himself and his family to the New World and established a town in Wisconsin named, with characteristic modesty, for himself. His interests prospered—the real estate and steamboat concerns, the farms where he raised Wisconsin's first field of hops and first flock of sheep. Only the vineyard failed so he left what was to become Sauk City behind him and made for San Diego, then a town whose population approached seven hundred on Sundays. California was "acquired" by the United States while he was en route. Getting himself elected sheriff almost at once, Haraszthy became judge and then state assemblyman before the vines on his farm had a chance to bear their first fruit. The new assemblyman soon moved the family to a new farm, Las Flores, located near San Francisco's Mission Dolores and went to work setting out more vines imported from Europe.

It was in February of 1852 that Haraszthy received a couple of bundles of cuttings he could not identify. The label, which he deciphered with difficulty, seemed to read "Zinfandel." Frank Schoonmaker has written " . . . if an absence of apparent ancestors is proof of divine origin certainly the Zinfandel grape is entitled to a whole collection of legends. Ampelographers have been able to arrive at any number of negative conclusions about it: the Zinfandel is *not* the German Zierfandler, it is not, as was long believed, the Hungarian Kadarka, it was *not* brought over from Europe under this name (Zinfandel)." And it is not found anywhere else in the world except in California. Though seldom large the vine is productive and its clusters are so compact that the grapes in the center of the bunch are

he discovers
Zinfandel

sometimes crushed. Zinfandel has been called California's own Beaujolais, and many among us find in it every virtue a wine should have. In popularity and sheer quantity of production, there is today no grape to rival it in the state. The good Colonel H. was never to know what a boon he had conferred upon his adopted land.

The Colonel seems to have restricted himself to strictly legal methods in his energetic efforts to raise capital. That at least was the conclusion of the courts after numerous trials, appeals and retrials in which Haraszthy was charged with embezzlement in connection with his stint as head of the San Francisco Mint. The lawsuits dragged on longer than the job had lasted, but neither political appointment nor public scandal diverted much of his attention from the acquisition of land and the planting of vines. By the marriage of his sons in 1863, he allied his family with that of California's last Spanish governor and foremost wine producer, General Mariano Vallejo. Eventually he owned the world's largest vineyard, six thousand acres of choice Sonoma countryside that he named Buena Vista. He built his family a fabulous Pompeian villa, entertained his distinguished neighbors, wrote a *Report on the Grapes and Wines of California* to please the State Agricultural Society, sent one of his sons to France to learn Champagne making and won prizes for his wines continuously at the State Fairs. Whereas other farmers employed Indian labor, Haraszthy brought one hundred and fifty Chinese up from San Francisco to work his vast holdings. They excavated deeper and deeper tunnels to be used as wine cellars and used the rock to build more stone vat houses for fermentation. Often when the heat of the day had been too oppressive, the pigtailed workmen could be seen plowing and dressing the vines in silence by the light of the moon.

By 1861 Haraszthy's prestige was such that the state legislature

marrying the
opposition's daughters

selected him to go to Europe to collect cuttings of vines and to learn all that he could about viticulture and winemaking and then to make it common

grape hunting knowledge in California. He left on his mission in June of that year and visited France, Italy, Switzerland, Spain and then Germany. At Johannisberg he confessed to Prince Metternich that his Excellency's Riesling was "of a perfection that as yet had no California peer." He brought back, in addition to his bales of notes, a dozen cart loads of fruit and nut trees and at least 200,000 cuttings of every imaginable sort of vine for the state to distribute for free throughout all the counties. All this work of collecting cost the Colonel nearly a year and twelve thousand dollars out of his own pocket. Because of his pro-Southern politics, however, the Legislature reneged on its promise to reimburse him and rejected the plants he'd gathered and the report he'd prepared as well. In 1946 the state set up a plaque commemorating Haraszthy's work; that is all the payment he ever received. He tried to distribute the vines himself. He envisioned California as the vineyard of the globe, a real utopia flowing with wine and honey, pheasant practically falling from the sky and casks of Zinfandel in every man's cellar. But he found it harder and harder to communicate this vision, and his projects began to fail.

He lost Buena Vista and then nearly lost his life when a boiler he was inspecting in his son's brandy distillery exploded practically in his face. At

end of a tycoon last he gave up the idea of re-establishing the Haraszthys in their noble and hereditary role of wine producers. His last venture was a sugar plantation in Nicaragua where he settled in 1869. Perhaps he intended to return to his beloved California where his sons carried on his name, but it was fated otherwise. One summer morning he left his house to search out a good site for a lumber mill and simply disappeared. It's claimed he was tracked as far as a large magnolia tree overhanging a stream whose waters were boiling with alligators. The trail is said to have ended there, causing his people to figure he'd fallen in trying to get across. Who knows? "He who plants a vine becomes entangled in its branches," wrote Flaubert we forget just where. Agoston Haraszthy, Count or Colonel, is only of historical interest to lovers of California's wine today (although there are still some convinced that thousands of ideally aged bottles of California's finest are waiting to be discovered when his hillside tunnels which collapsed during the 1906 tremor are completely excavated). More than any man, he managed to adapt the technique of the Old World vineyards and winemasters to the untested *his legacy* climate and virgin soil of California. His monument is the Zinfandel. More than anyone else, it is Haraszthy California must thank for its present-day position in the world of wine.

Little more than a century after his death, California could already boast nearly thirty thousand active vineyards and about three hundred fifty commercial wineries. Few counties in the state have no winery at all, and together these wineries account for approximately 6 percent of the world's annual wine production.

By the time of Haraszthy's unheralded death, a scourge had descended on the wine lands of the Old and New Worlds alike. In Portugal it first appeared in 1868; by the following year it had reached Bordeaux; it spread swiftly everywhere. By the mid-1870's European wine production *the plague* had fallen off at least 50 percent, and it must have seemed that wine would soon be only a memory. The tiny aphid-type insects devouring the roots of the vines resisted every conceivable remedy. The *Phylloxera* had come from America and so, eventually, did the cure in the form of native American vine stocks which were found to be immune to the root louse. The devastation was unparalleled in agricultural history and required incredible toil to repair.

Virtually all the vines of the world have been grafted on to the roots of native American grapes ever since and *Phylloxera* is all but unknown today. The threat persisted, however, until 1971, when University of California scientists announced a new way of preventing *Phylloxera* which does not necessitate the time and toil of grafting.

California suffered relatively less damage than the other wine lands from the *Phylloxera;* it was the hand of man that nearly put an end to wine production in this country. Prohibition, the "Noble Experiment," went into effect in 1919 and for fourteen years thereafter a legal drought lay upon the land. The authorities permitted a handful of wineries to continue to operate making altar wines; Concannon and Beaulieu were among the fortunate few. The law also allowed home production of up to two hundred gallons of wine *legal plague* per annum, and most vineyards were reduced to shipping their grapes East to satisfy this demand. The better varieties of wine grape did not withstand the rigors of shipment, being thin-skinned and fragile. Fine wine grapes are, in any case, attractive neither to the mouth nor the eye of any but a vine-yardist, and so the Rieslings, Cabernets, Pinots and others were uprooted and replaced by the high-yielding mediocre types like Carignane, Thompson Seedless and Alicante Bouschet. In 1929 some eight hundred carloads of this potential California red were shipped from Napa County alone. Since the profession of making wine was outlawed, the men who did it were forced into other fields. The tanks and casks that grow more precious with time and are the pride of the vintner's heart were sold or abandoned to a long and sad *dry times* emptiness which few survived. Dry rot and the spider ruled the wineries undisturbed, except by an occasional roar like the roll of artillery as the irreplaceable cooperage collapsed. Worst of all was the effect of Prohibition on the public's taste. By 1930 America was consuming about 140,000 gallons of domestic "wine" per year, according to the estimates of the government's dry enforcement bureau. This was nearly twice the amount of wine that all the grapes in the country could have produced! Bootleggers had learned to make as much as six or seven hundred gallons of "wine" from a single ton of grapes by fermenting sugar and water on the skins after they had already been pressed dry. The stuff was red, alcoholic and available: people forgot how good wine tasted.

The wreckage of the wine industry that Prohibition wrought required not years but decades to repair. Quality wines could not be produced until the vineyards had been replanted, new cooperage acquired, and experienced winemakers found. Even after good and occasionally fine domestic wines became available, it was years and years before enough consumers acquired the critical experience necessary to care what they were drinking and create a market for quality. Except for the war years, the wine industry throughout the nation was far from prosperous until 1960 or so. Prohibition was really an experiment in barbarism. Incarnate civilization and its blood would be wine. No liquid flows more incessantly through the labyrinth of symbols we have conceived to mark our status as human beings.

modern barbarity

We have equally moronic forms of Prohibition now, though hopefully Americans will not be prohibited wine, at least, again. But musing on the future of fine wine in this country as recently as 1968, Mr. Alex Waugh could still wonder if there were sound business reasons why the hunt for those rare places that can produce exceptional vintages should continue. The omnibibulous Mr. Waugh has long since had his answer. Extensive prospecting for new vineyards in California has begun to pay off on a grand scale. Today, wines from Mendocino, Lake and Monterey counties are commanding the same respect that has hitherto been reserved for those of the

vineyard prospecting

Napa and Livermore valleys. "It may take us a hundred years to find out where these wines should be planted in California," wrote Colonel Haraszthy in the report he presented along with the grape cuttings he brought back from Europe. His estimate was optimistic. It took much longer than that for Spain to find its lone Sherry region or for France to locate its Clos de Vougeot. It may be several centuries yet before the Californian *terroir* is exhaustively prospected.

prospects and retrospects

The vast new plantings have heavily favored the best varieties of grapes. Consider only Cabernet Sauvignon, California's reputedly best and positively most expensive red. At the end of World War II well under 1,000 acres of this varietal existed in the entire state. A quarter century later, by 1970, there were over 6,000. In 1980 California will have better than 26,000 acres of Cabernet Sauvignon to harvest. In other words, there'll be more than four times more of California's finest red available than was made in 1970. Consider her noblest white likewise, the celebrated Chardonnay. Some 1,500 acres were bearing in 1970; by '80 that figure will exceed 13,000—an increase, roughly speaking, from 400,000 to over two and a half million cases of wine.

Our recent wine boom has lost its news value, but this will not lessen its effects. We've barely begun to feel them, in fact. With the confidence of a man whose predictions are soon surpassed, the author of *The Wines of America,* Mr. Leon Adams, foresees wine consumption in this country reaching "at least five gallons per capita by the end of the century." That's as much as a German drinks, speaking statistically, and approximately treble our current intake. In social and cultural terms it's also the fulfillment of a long cherished dream of America.

what's coming soon

Thomas Jefferson was not alone among our founding fathers in hoping that this country might become a nation of wine drinkers. The word "alcoholism" was yet to be coined when he wrote: "I consider it a great error to consider a heavy tax on wine as a tax on luxury. No nation is drunken where wine is cheap; and none sober where the dearness of wine substitutes ardent spirits as the common beverage." Time and science have confirmed his observation and at last the time to try his remedy has come. Wine is an "ally" in the pursuit of happiness, as any Don Juan can tell you, and you don't need a guru to be initiated into its mysteries. California, as everybody knows, is bringing forth an abundance, a geyser of wine. Enough to transform feeding into dining for millions and millions more Americans. Enough even to civilize our national drinking habits. More than enough to tempt wine lovers with different delights every night of the year. What stands in the way of all this is the pyramid of extortionate taxes and costly red tape that straitjacket wine distribution. This is the only reason good wine for day-to-day drinking has to cost more than milk. And not until it's easily affordable for all will our American wine revolution be won.

a geyser of wine

With this revolution barely under way, one truth is already self-evident: devout wine bibbers go forth and multiply at a phenomenal rate. It's easy to forget that most of the wine made and sold in this country before 1967 was, to be blunt, the cheapest sort of stuff to get drunk on. The winos far outnumbered the wine bibbers in the land right up until that year when—for the first time and almost overnight—Americans discovered wine. Sales of cheap 14- to 20-percent alcohol dessert wines have declined by almost one-fifth since then, and our mealtime consumption of dry table wines has more than tripled. With all due respect for faddism, this is clear proof of what a contagious pleasure wine is and why from now on out, its

Americans discover it

devotees will only increase in number unless, as always predicted, California really does sink beneath the sea. It's going to be a wonderfully vinous meantime. As we hope this book will show, we are entering the Golden Age of Californian wine.

Now when it comes to California wines, it is only fair to warn you *nota bene* you are dealing with fanatics, the writer not least among them. Perhaps you should read no further. As with any trip, yoga, ufology, or women's liberation, say, you become part of the phenomenon just by taking an interest in it. As an average citizen, five or six of your annual eight bottles of wine come from California as it is. This is because virtually all of our country's fine wines come from Northern California and the state as a whole *California's contribution* produces over 75 percent of all the wine we drink. Ever obedient to the first principle of omnibibulosity, we drink it because it is there—or rather *from here.* It's ours, what this land of ours produces, what we provide ourselves. But indulging your curiosity where these native nectars are concerned entails the risk of exceeding your national quota, for the only way to learn more about America's wine is to drink more of it.

It's difficult to write about wine without gradually lapsing into lyricism, geography and French. More difficult still is it to grasp, just from reading, exactly what a writer's effusions are really about: you cannot taste the cold, printed page. This is clearly the reason, as the blessed Saintsbury *vinous verities* lamented, "Wine has been stinted of its due literary sizings." But since along with women and song it ranks as one of life's three great joys, people will carry on about it and there is at least one good reason for paying some attention when they do. *The price on a bottle of wine has practically nothing to do with the quality of what's inside it.* A little book learning can save a lot of money, in short, and is therefore not to be despised. If the

exploring

writer also reports marvels of vinous *volupté* you've never suspected, don't be tempted to question his sobriety at once. Call Marco Polo to mind and reserve your judgement. Marco Polo, as everybody knows, not only told stories that made contemporary Italians scoff—he also introduced them to pasta. Here then, together with some reflections, much secondhand information and an occasional burst of ill temper, is a true and faithful relation of fifteen years enchantment with California wines.

WINE TALK
What are you trying to tell me?

When one says 'He gave a name to his sensations' one forgets that a great deal of stage setting in the language is presupposed if the mere act of naming is to make sense.

—Ludwig Wittgenstein

t is said of the French diplomat Talleyrand that he only once reproached a guest for not showing the proper respect due some particularly fine vintage. "I would willingly do so if only you would show me how, sire," his embarrassed table companion replied. "First you must hold your glass to the light and swirl the wine slowly to study its color." "Yes?" "Then you bring the glass to your nose to breathe the wine's bouquet." "And then?" "And then, young man, you set your glass down and you talk about it."

Talking about wine has ever been one of the many pleasures this ancient and divine drink affords those who love it. That is why this book about wine is being written.

Of all the curious actions of which our mere bodies are capable, the two that most readily fire the imagination are making love and drinking wine. Talking about wine can sometimes make us feel the way we did as adolescents discussing sex—unwilling to seem totally ignorant but hesitant to express ourselves freely lest we discover ourselves in the company of someone who "knows all about it." Nobody does, of course, and eventually we realize why nobody ever could. Some subjects are inexhaustible. Such animals as the wine "expert" do exist, however, and we shall never know as much as those makers, merchants and tasters who spend all their time with wine. They are experts, and the expertise goes along with their profession. But we amateurs need offer no apology for our opinions so long as we are worthy of that noble name. Obscured though its basic meaning has become in present English usage, the word "amateur" is descended from the Latin

experts and amateurs

verb *amo,* "I love." The wine expert must make wine his livelihood, but the "amateur" is a lover of wine for its own sake.

Webster's notwithstanding, the wine connoisseur does not need to be a wine expert, and neither does the wine bibber need to be a connoisseur. We are all perfectly competent to judge what pleases us and what does not in *connoisseurship* entertainment, food and drink. After all, your taste is as uniquely your own as your fingerprints are. If you have drunk enough wine to discover a preference for some—and perhaps a distaste for others—you are already in the ranks of the world's wine bibbers. The rightful object of all learning is enjoyment, and one gradually learns to distinguish different degrees of pleasure. To know what you mean when you call one movie or steak "good" and another "great" is to pass a critical judgement based on past experience and this is the essence of connoisseurship. It's not a word to attach too much importance to. As you unconsciously absorb knowledge, make comparisons and discover circumstances in which you prefer this wine to that over the years, you become by degrees a connoisseur. As your taste continues to develop, you probably also raise your standards of taste and appreciation. In time your friends may consider that your love of wine has led you to adopt strange, esoteric practices and to mutter mystic formulae while you drink. You must try to explain that like any other esthetic creation, like poetry, painting, music or dance, the more you come to know about wine, the more you find in it to enjoy. Tell them about Talleyrand.

M. de Talleyrand—if it was really he and not another responsible for *wine slang* our anecdote—was no crackpot. He was an Experienced Connoisseur showing a novice how to make the most of one of the gods' greatest gifts. Terms like "bouquet" are just part of the slang of wine lore. In every specialized thing we do, be it fencing, fishing or car theft, there are specialized terms. Wine makers and wine drinkers have theirs too.

Now some unfortunates drink labels instead of wine. They always notice a wine's faults before finding any virtues in it, and they are always especially careful to lace their comments liberally with wine slang to impress you. James Thurber epitomized this dread disorder, wine snobbery, in his memorable cartoon, "It's a naive domestic Burgundy without any breeding, but I think you'll be amused by its presumption."

Such pretentious people are not hard to recognize, and their misuse of wine slang should not blind us to its value. A word like "breeding" need not be affectation; it actually has a fairly definite meaning. A good Gamay Beaujolais may boast a dozen excellent qualities, not the least of which is its moderate price. Taste it, however, after a Margaux or a first-rate Cabernet Sauvignon and it is not difficult to sense that these wines are clothed in a certain unaggressive elegance to which the forthright Gamay makes no claim. The word "breeding" expresses it exactly. Tell your friends to beware of over-hasty headshaking if they hear you using such language. Why should the man who tells you in detail about his customized automobile expect rapt attention and yet consider you a suspicious character should you fondly recollect your last Lafite-Rothschild? The car's body cannot compare with the Claret's, and obsolescence is built into the one as longevity is built into the other. Ah well, perhaps it's sometimes better to be silent; you don't want to come on like your neighbor with his comparative history of the major-league shortstops over the past twenty seasons.

"And Noah began to be an husbandman, and he planted a vineyard . . . ." Presumably he had opportunity to compare his own product with that of other wineries, for *Genesis* later assures us that " . . . Noah lived

the communication question

after the Flood three hundred and fifty years." The name by which he called the gift of the grape probably sounded much like our own word "wine." At least the Hittites, whose language was dominant in the Mount Ararat neighborhood as early as 1500 B.C. referred to it in their hieroglyphic script as *uin-*. *Woi-ne-wei* occurs as the word for wine merchant in Mycenean Greek; in Archaic Greek wine is *woinos,* which loses its W to become *oinos* in classical times. The W sound was retained in the Etruscan and Latin derivative *vinum* (V sounding like W in Latin) and its offshoots, *vino, vin, wein,* and *wine.* The Hittite term found its way into other neighboring languages—*gini* in Armenian and *gvino* in Georgian—and was adopted into the Semitic tongues also, becoming in Hebrew *vayin* and remaining as *wa-yn* in Arabic today. (We are indebted to Professor Charles Seltman's *Wine in the Ancient World* for this fascinating piece of *viniana.*) If music is the international language, wine, historically, has been the international word.

the word "wine"

"De gustibus non disputandum est," wrote Horace. "Taste is nothing to argue over." The poet's sagacious suggestion grates against human nature, particularly the nature of the world's wine lovers who continue to honor it only in the breach. We may be sure that men were disputing the imagined merits of various wines in this country long before they produced America's first wine in 1564 from grapes that were growing wild in Florida. Now wines made from native American grapes are so different from any others that comparisons would be absurd. Their devotees are content to quote Longfellow's

Eastern American wines

> But Catawba Wine
> Has a taste more divine,
> More dulcet, delicious, and dreamy . . . .

and thus justified, to ignore, almost or utterly, all other wines whatsoever.

Native American grapes belong to the *labrusca* family and are mainly raised in the Eastern part of the United States. This Eastern wine industry is centered in New York and Ohio, but has vineyards in the South and Midwest and elsewhere.

The completely separate Californian industry supplies some 75 to 80 percent of our domestic wines. Californian and European wines are blood relatives, so to speak, for both come from grapes belonging to the *vinifera* or "winebearer" family. The California progeny of the European varieties are brought up under the very different conditions of the five growing regions in that state and produce wines with a character all their own, reminiscent but *California wines* not imitative of European. The time is long past when Californians need feel the least defensive about the quality of their wines. Quoth, for one, Mr. Hugh Johnson, one of our most eminent authorities on all matters vinous: "Of all the vineyards of the New World, California is the one which has suffered most discouragement . . . and yet the one which makes the best wine. Of the other new lands of the vine you can say that many of their wines are good and some fine. Of California you can say that many of her wines are fine and some great." Today he'd have to say "many great."

Where a vine is planted is the most important single factor deter-mining the quality of the wine it produces and the specific *goût de terroir* or *"terroir"* taste of ground it has. If one insists upon making comparisons, it is possible, even instructive, to compare California's Rieslings with the wines of the Rhine, Cabernet Sauvignon with Bordeaux, and so forth—so long as you don't expect one to be a copy of the other. Now many people whose palates are habituated to Old World wine flavors set up European wines, probably *comparisons* unconsciously, as a standard against which they measure all others. They tend to class these others as good or bad in direct proportion to the degree to which they imitate European wines. For example, Creighton Churchill, Esq. writes of French sparkling Burgundy: "The only thing to recommend it, as opposed to its California or New York State cousins, is that it is at least made of Old World grapes on Old World soil—and thus its taste carries a certain hint of Old World *'terroir'*." We find very little to recommend any sparkling Burgundy but then . . . *"De gustibus non disputandum est."*

We have strayed from our topic. M. de Talleyrand would not have us set our glasses down and declare allegiance to one or another wine-producing region, which would be folly in any case. No, you talk about the wine before you because it is the nature of wine to make one talk. It is also interesting because our sensations are so personal and subjective. A wine he considers "light" you may find as full of body as Homer. Furthermore, a fine wine has such a complex character that different tasters may be struck more by one element than by another, depending upon what each is most sensitive to. There's truth in the old proverb "In water you see your own face, in wine the heart of another." To talk about what you feel, what you discover and enjoy, is to reveal yourself and take another into your confidence. Wine loosens the tongue at the same time it maketh glad the heart. But to share, to compare and analyze the subtle, fleeting impressions a wine produces is not only to communicate with another but to discover for oneself what, exactly, those impressions are. The qualities and precise sensations we perceive must be crystallized into words or they are soon lost to us and easily forgotten. If you're called upon for an opinion of a wine you find mediocre or unpleasant, it is of course better not to talk than to give offense. You can always confine yourself to a laconic "interesting" and still be telling the truth. After all, it is interesting to taste wines one dislikes if only to know what not to buy for oneself.

talking about wine

*what wine
has to say*

But part of any pleasure comes from discussing it, and to character-ize and compare sensations which exist in a realm where no word has ever entered, we are compelled to invent a language that draws upon vocabulary used in other fields and to speak in images and symbols. You may, if you like, free your fantasy and find in your wine the shavings of cherubs' wings, the glory of a tropic dawn, the red clouds of sunsets or fragments of lost epics by dead masters. If you pay attention to it, a good wine will always have something to tell you. What exactly it says no one can ever completely understand, of course, and that is wine's charm and its mystery. But bursts of lyricism are not always necessary to describe what you prefer in today's Burgundy to the one you drank last week. It's really no more difficult than telling someone why, say, you think *Amarcord* Fellini's greatest film. There are no authorities in matters of taste, and there's no danger of appearing ridiculous so long as your similes don't appear in print. To find André Simon calling a wine "a girl of fifteen coming in on tiptoes" on the cold printed page may well make us smile. But had we been there, glass in hand, to share that bottle with him, no doubt we should have known what he meant at once. No doubt, too, he would have wanted to hear what we thought of it.

ordinaire

Not all wines deserve discussion. The wines that serve as everyday drink may call for an "I like it" or "The wine is all right," and that's all there is to that. At least four-fifths and maybe more of the world's wine production is made to be consumed within a year of fermentation. This completely anonymous wine is what the French call *vin ordinaire*. Having no word for it in English, we've borrowed the French term and usually call it *ordinaire* ourselves. Most of our American *ordinaires* are generic wines—blends named, that is, after European prototypes like Burgundy, Chablis, Rhine *und so weiter*. (Varietal wines are those named after the grape variety from which they are made. More on this later.) *Ordinaire* is not always made by trolls and need not be repulsive to the palate—much of it is gulpable enough. It simply lacks any kind of character by which to distinguish one from another.

When we come to good wine we begin to have something to talk about. What do you mean when you say a dish is good? What makes a new song good? We must include here everything from just plain well made on upwards. Good wine is true to type and cannot be mistaken for anything except what it says it is. If it's labelled Zinfandel and tastes no different from Burgundy to you, you may be sure you're drinking *ordinaire*. Furthermore, good wine is sufficiently individualistic to be worth tasting with some attention. In other words, it's not just drinkable, it's interesting. Much of the California generic wine labelled as to county of origin falls into this category and a good deal of her varietal wine as well. Good covers the whole field between *ordinaire* and fine wines. Good wine is nothing to rave about, but it is something to be thankful for.

good

Fine wine, on the other hand, is a blessing. These are the bottles which may lack greatness, but are much more than merely good. It is safe to say that the acknowledged fine wines of North America come almost exclusively from Northern California. Fine wine can only be produced from certain grape varieties cultivated on ground that has the ideal chemical properties for that wine grape, the best exposure to the sun and just the right amount of rainfall, in addition to protection from winds and frosts. There are not too many of these places to be found on the globe. They produce wine that is not simply alive, it's lively. Whereas good wine may be interesting, fine wine is exciting. Every so often you discover a fine California generic wine like the BV Burgundy of 1968 we remember so fondly (along with a number of others), but the great majority of fine California wines are

fine

varietals. There will be more and more of it now that Americans almost overnight have "discovered" the wonder of fine wine. Those wines a producer takes greatest pride in almost always carry the highest allowable appellation— "produced and bottled by . . . ." (and sometimes "estate-bottled" just for good measure), and they often, though by no means invariably, bear a vintage date. Let's postpone our discussion of vintage until later. The only sure test of a wine's quality is the taste of the wine; there are fine wines that are not famous, and famous wines that are not fine.

No vineyard or district in the world invariably produces great wine, for great wine is a miracle, the rare result of a perfect collaboration between man and nature under perfect conditions. These are the Nureyevs of the world of wine. It is even more difficult to generalize about the quality of greatness in wines than to draw the line between the fine and the great. All great wines differ from one another, having only their nobility in common. Their respective virtues may be debated, but each wine in this, our smallest category, is superb and each unique. The aftertaste of a great wine is just as complex, harmonious and delightful as the first whiff of its bouquet, and everything it has to offer is equally perfect. The experience of great wine is something every wine bibber should enjoy at least once a lifetime, if only to find out what all the fuss is about. We have every confidence we shall retain in the hereafter a clear recollection of certain great wines it has been our good fortune to encounter this go-round. Alexandre Dumas said you should drink Montrachet, the white Burgundy, only on your knees with your hat off. That's the way a great wine makes you feel.

We would only add there should be some one to share the experience with, for it is painful to have to keep such pleasure to oneself.

WINE TASTING
How do you know it's any good?

It is true that taste can be educated. It is also true that taste can be perverted . . . . If any man gives you a wine you can't bear, don't say it is beastly . . . but don't say you like it. You are endangering your soul and the use of wine as well. Seek out some other wine good to your taste.

—Hilaire Belloc

asting requires intelligence of the body as well as the mind. The sense of hearing is the only one of the five recognized senses which does not come into play in wine tasting, and even here there are poets to protest the contrary. Baudelaire is by no means the only one who sometimes thought he heard the soul of wine singing. There are others, including even Englishmen like old W. E. "Invictus" Henley.

> The spirit of wine sang in my glass and
> I hastened with love to this odorous music,
> His flushed and magnificent song.

Who can be sure whether or not Henley means us to take him literally? Certainly we shall not insist that wines never sing to those who love them, but most of us know only the sound they make gurgling into our glasses. "The wine experience," so to speak, begins with our visual sensa-
sight tions: the first thing that strikes us about a wine is its color. Red, rosé, white, each with its infinite range of shades. Red wines are often deep purple when new; some that have aged a long time turn the color of terra-cotta tiles. California rosés often show a distinct tinge of orange or may be almost red sometimes. Whites can be practically colorless, tending perhaps toward a very pale green; some show the glint of old gold. The French refer to a
"gown" wine's color as its "gown." Like a log fire or a candle flame, the animation and beauty of a wine's color in the glass can induce long reveries if you let it. Experience alone teaches what color characteristics are more or less appropriate to the different types of wine.

Lifting the glass by its stem and looking through it at a source of light, whether simply the whiteness of the tablecloth or an electric light or whatever, enables you to perceive the wine's brilliancy, that is to say, its clarity. Most commercial wines are filtered before shipment to insure that they reach the consumer in a brilliant condition. More and more of our finest wines are left in their "natural" state, so to speak, and not subjected *sediment* to fining and/or filtration at all. Others receive the lightest possible such treatment. Perhaps the clarity is imperfect. This is not a sign of negligence on the part of the bottler nor does it mean there's anything wrong with the wine. In fact, a few knowledgeable wine lovers will not buy an old red which has no sediment in the bottle. When it exists it is a simple matter to pour the wine into a new bottle after the sediment has been allowed to settle, taking care in your handling and uncorking of the bottle not to stir it up again. Do not worry if a little sediment slips into your glass—it is not dirt and, being usually odorless and tasteless, will not pollute the wine's taste. At most you may feel something like a little dust on the tongue. It is not serious. Allow the wine to sit still a few moments in the glass and even this can be avoided—unless you down it in a gulp like medicine.

There is another element that can be revealed to the sight if one *"legs"* wants to look at the "legs" of the wine in his glass. When the glass is twirled and the wine then comes to rest again, the thin film of wine covering the wall of the glass forms into heavy transparent tears which slowly trickle down the curve of the crystal and leave behind them long trails that French wine tasters call the "legs" of the wine. There's a knack involved in swirling the wine in the glass without sloshing any out of it. Such a catastrophe can be avoided if the glass is half full or less and the aspiring leg watcher has practiced his twirl. The legs are the signs of a wine's richness. You can deduce the degree of maturity, of "fatness" and unctuousness to come according to whether the legs are plentiful and dense or few and spaced out. Not all wines have legs to show, but with some, shorter legs follow the first ones and the glass will weep unendingly.

While the wine has been delighting the eye it has had time to breathe; now the nose can enjoy the splendors it has to offer. Authorities on the subject claim the human olfactory sense can distinguish between four-thousand and ten-thousand different odors. The odors of the grapes from which the wine was made are called "aromas." Thus any Pinot Chardonnay should have the characteristic Pinot Chardonnay aroma, and with a little practice you can learn to recognize it. The aroma is the part of the smell that you can expect. There are also odors that come from the processing or aging of the wine, and these constitute its bouquet. Many factors may result in widely different bouquets among several brands of the same wine. It takes time for a wine to develop bouquet, and you can never predict precisely what it will be like. Of course cheap wines will often smell so bad that it's pretentious to speak of aroma or bouquet at all—"fumes" is more like it.

smell

aroma and bouquet

Perfumes are heavier than air and will therefore collect in the top of the glass; filling the glass to the brim merely wastes the wine's delectable fragrance. Just sniff the wine to begin with and see if you can smell *anything.* Exhale completely to free your nostrils of the odor, and go back for another sniff. Pay attention to your sensations and you will probably discover something new that you missed at first. If the wine is good, there is a haunting compound of clean, fresh smells all bound together by a firm sweetness. No water drinker can imagine how many different sweetnesses there can be!

Now that you have made the acquaintance of this complex odor, it is time to get to know it well. Stick your nose into the glass and inhale very slowly and steadily. What now fills your head cannot be described as anything but a bouquet—a combination of all the perfumes in their full force. Very few wines are as wonderful as their smell, so linger over it as long as you like. Return to the bouquet again and again as you drink to see how it *"frozen" bouquet* develops with increasing warmth and oxidation. If the wine is served chilled, the bouquet may be "frozen" until the wine has warmed enough to release it. Dry whites and rosés, indeed most young wines, seem to have a certain fruity odor which can be attributed more to their youth and freshness than to the smell of the grape. If you are unable to detect much of a bouquet, it may be because the wine is too young or simply too "little," as they say, to have one. More rarely, the body of the wine may smother its odors, so that the nose has no way of suspecting the surprises in store for the palate.

It's just possible all this wine smelling may turn up some unpleasant discoveries; you must expect to encounter off-odors from time to time. *off-odors* Yeasty odors that should have disappeared during early aging sometimes don't. Or maybe the vintner was overenthusiastic in using sulphur-dioxide gas to prevent the development of harmful bacteria during the fermentation of the wine and it reeks of sulphur. This is most often noticed in whites and is a particularly nasty defect. Occasionally you may find a wine, particularly a red that's been bottled for a number of years, "corky." This is an *corkiness* indescribable but unmistakable moldiness that pervades both the odor and the taste of the wine, but unlike the previous defects, it's something you can put up with. Especially if it's the only wine in the house and it's raining out of doors. "Corkiness" is also the one quality that the greatest and least of wines sometimes have in common. The only other redeeming thing about it is that it is one of nature's unexplained mysteries—something to do with neurotic cork oaks, but nobody's sure quite what.

Now that you've listened to, looked at and smelled of the wine, it's finally time to take your first taste of it. But don't be hasty: the number of different sensations your tongue is about to undergo is in no way related to *taste* the amount of wine you can get into your mouth. The taste buds are not equally distributed in there. Most are on the tip and sides, with the remainder concentrated at the very back of the tongue. To begin with take only a sip, little more than a few drops of the wine, and roll it around to reach all these zones. It's as if the aroma of the wine becomes suddenly tangible as you hold this first sip in your mouth taking careful note of what the wine is trying to tell you. How dry is it? How acid? How astringent? Are all the various odor/flavors as harmonious in the mouth as they were in the *sipping* nose? You may want to take several little sips, concentrating on a different element each time.

Most wines reveal their deepest secret, the "central" taste standing out over the others, at first contact. But the flavor of wine is as complex as its chemistry, and if the wine is fine its flavor will be many-layered, each component present individually and at the same time blended into a perfect whole. As with the bouquet, the taste of a wine oftentimes changes and develops as a bottle is consumed, and a wine one first judged to lack character may improve by being better known. Just as smells and tastes intermingle and sometimes merge altogether, the sensations we experience upon first tasting a wine are an almost imperceptible mingling of a number of different qualities. The challenge lies in perceiving these nuances. Wine-making is more an art than a science, and wine is made to be loved and not

simply drunk. To love it you have to appreciate its true character and for this, drinking is not enough; you must taste.

There are various tricks that tasters use to bring out the flavors in that first sip or two of wine. Some people hold a little on the tip of the tongue and suck air in over it. Others hold a like amount on the back of the tongue, open their mouths, and exhale over it. Either technique requires a little practice, and even then the chances are your gurgling will sound like faulty plumbing. The theory behind such carrying on is that aerating the wine *nella bocca* reveals any hidden aromas, and probably it does. If you find such a procedure has value, therapeutic or otherwise, there's no reason not to use it. But if it doesn't look good to you, or makes you self-conscious, you need not worry about missing anything as long as you taste attentively. What you do with the wine in your mouth is your business: the only affectation is to spit it out.

The sense of touch also comes into play when you put anything in your mouth, and in evaluating or trying to describe the "feel" of a wine you must speak of its "body." The alcohol in the wine always produces a slightly burning sensation, though a "well-built" wine never feels hot. Body has to do with alcohol, therefore, but also with the wine's robustness or fullness of texture, the weight of the wine on your tongue. A rich red Pinot Noir or Barbera would seem somehow deficient if it were not obviously "full-bodied"–almost substantial enough to chew sometimes. A Gamay Beaujolais of similar consistency, on the other hand, would seem too thick, too "heavy-bodied"; such reds are meant to be lighter. Most white wines are even more light-bodied than any red, if you will permit an overly broad generalization. Looking at a wine's legs gives you a hint in advance as to how "fat" or how "thin" the body will prove to be. There is another trick of tasting that allows even finer discrimination, and this is to bring the wine into contact with the entire lining of the mouth and then press the tongue against the palate. You'll readily discover whether the wine has more the feel and consistency of water or of oil. We examine our sips in every way we can think of, interrogate our senses, and then the wine gets swallowed. The disappearance of the wine is not, however, the end of the pleasure we receive from it; there remains the aftertaste. Often this can be the most dazzling part of the whole experience, as you are suddenly left with an awareness of all

aftertaste sorts of lingering fragrances that permeate the mouth and nose. You not only discover qualities that had hitherto gone unnoticed, but you are all at once reminded of each separate sensation leading up to this "finish," as the aftertaste is also sometimes called. A "little" wine, a "simple" wine, may have no more aftertaste than it has bouquet. Such a wine, that has not much to tell us and says it all at once, is said to "cut short its taste." With a fine wine the taste may stay on and on, as if to assure us our pleasures are no less real for being transitory.

We hasten to add, it takes much less time to do all these things than to read about them. However you go about it, the important thing is that you not simply fill your mouth and swallow, but rather pay attention to the wine the way you might taste a dish to see whether it needs more seasoning. And what makes this trouble worthwhile? A fair and philosophical question: Why? The satisfaction in wine tasting comes, not from finding fault with inferior wines, but from sharpening our senses, which is to say, cultivating our taste in the most basic meaning of that term. The idea is not just to enjoy but to make the most of that enjoyment. Too often we look without seeing, hear without listening, or—drink without tasting, surely the greatest insult you can offer a fine wine. It seems a waste indeed to pass up pleasures that can be ours in exchange for nothing more than attentiveness and concentration. These are faculties a taster exercises, and since anything one pays close attention to stays in the memory, he soon develops the ability to remember his sensations. M. André Malraux calls the works of art engraved in memory our "imaginary museums." Over the course of a lifetime we also stock our "imaginary wine cellars," for as Robert Louis Stevenson observed, "A bottle of good wine, like a good act, shines ever in the retrospect." Memory is the only paradise from which we cannot be driven, and wine creates memories for us. It makes us happy now and again twenty years from now by the memory of it. But we depend upon today's impressions for our memories tomorrow. These bottles, some plain and some precious, that lie asleep but still alive in the past, amply reward the taster for every respect he showed them.

"le musée imaginaire"

   You don't have to be a fine connoisseur or greatly gifted or to have practiced tasting at your mother's knee in order to derive the greatest pleasures from tasting wines. The first wines one learns to enjoy are almost always ones that are easily recognized and understood. Sweetness always flatters the palate, and the tip of the tongue is the part most sensitive to it. Probably this explains why all of us know exactly how much sugar we like in our coffee and usually can tell whether that exact amount was exceeded even a little. Also for this reason the first wines people turn on to are often the flowery, slightly sweet whites like Green Hungarian and Chenin Blanc. In time one begins looking for greater subtlety and richness in wine, as in music or anything else. The sour-sensing taste buds lie along the edges of the tongue and the bitter-sensitive ones across the back. The progression in taste is generally said to follow this order also. One learns to enjoy and appreciate drier, tart white wines after the first not-so-dry ones and lastly the

sweet, sour, bitter

astringent, dry and faintly bitter reds. This at least is how the professors have it figured, though we really doubt that anything so logical can be true. Still it is a fact that it usually takes time to acquire new tastes and discover one's personal preferences. After all, the only taste we're born with is one for mother's milk and every other taste we have has been acquired sometime! *"acquired" tastes*   Certainly it is only with time that the wine bibber becomes familiar with what to be sensitive to and learns what to look for in different wines. Although one's liking for wine can come with the first glass, you come to understand and appreciate it more and more with time and experience.

As in lovemaking, reading is a damned poor substitute for experience in the gentle art of tasting. It is one of those things you find out about for yourself. And despite its genteel associations, wine appreciation is no attainment; it's a pleasure and a game. If you wonder what we mean, get two similar wines and pour two glasses of one and a third glass of the other. You may number the glasses and shuffle them, or ask a friend to pour for you, so *the tasting game*   long as you do not know which wine goes into which glass but have a way of keeping track. Then see if you can pick out the odd glass of wine. Your chances of guessing correctly are one in three, so the experiment should be repeated at least three times in a row. For best results rinse your mouth or chew a bit of bread and allow a few moments between wines. You will be surprised at how many differently delicious wines you can learn to recognize. You will remember the names easily once the tastes get fixed in your mind. It takes time for a taster to become familiar with what to look for and what to be sensitive to. A familiarity with wine aromas and flavors comes not so much through extensive as comparative sampling. Only by tasting one wine against another can we learn how to discriminate between them. The more we are able to discriminate, the better shall we be able to appreciate

the finer points of what is set before us. Nearly seven-and-a-half-billion gallons of wine are consumed every year in this world, and you can try out our tasting game with any of it. The better the wine is, of course, the more enjoyable the game becomes. Which is the better of any two similar wines? The one you prefer, certainly. And what's the difference between them? There isn't any if you can't find it.

Tis a pity wine should be so deleterious
For tea and coffee leave us much more serious.

–George Gordon Lord Byron

wine craze and its symptoms

You can be sure somebody's become a certified wine nut the day he starts to keep a cellar book or wine diary, though you can't be sure he'll admit to the seriousness of this symptom. Wine nuts are funny. All they actually have in those scrapbooks is dates and names of drinking companions, collages of raggedy old labels they steamed off bottles, stains and adjectives—delicate, racy, mild, noble, elegant, fruity, slender, harmonious, angular, unfinished, powerful, developed, dry, bitter, green, pure, earthy, ripe, masculine, soft, obtrusive, liquorous, stony, flattering, full, nutty, nervy, flat, strong, piquant, spicy, steely, characterless, fiery, flinty, blunt, . . . all sorts of words like that. Not, mind you, that your wine nut really trusts words! Wine shows that things are not all so comprehensible and expressible as we are led to believe, and most words come down to more or less happy misunderstandings.

WINE BUYING
What are you looking for?

I do not, however, think the attempt to tell mankind of these matters a good thing, except in the case of some few who are capable of discovering the truth for themselves with a little guidance.

—Plato

uying any kind of wine should be an occasion for directing dark thoughts at Washington and other government centers. Only the most expensive cost more per gallon to produce than milk. Wine costs what it costs because of a pyramid of Federal, state and local taxes which amount to several times the value of the product. Portugal has no excise tax on wine, which is generally cheaper there than beer. The Spanish pay less for their *ordinaire* than for their bottled drinking water! The general availability

wine as food

and wide use of wine in this country will be curtailed as long as it is looked upon as an alcoholic beverage instead of as a food. There's no more fitting occasion for a lover of wine to lift his voice in protest against such a miserable state of affairs than the beginning of a chapter like this.

The wisest piece of advice in Hilaire Belloc's little book called *Advice* is indubitably this: "Divide your buying of wine into two clear departments (1) Buying ordinary wine. (2) Buying special wine." Accordingly, we'll put off till later considering the few undeniably great wines and the many fine ones and concentrate first on the search for the best wine for day-to-day drinking. Like the quest for the perfect hamburger, this is a search that can continue *ad infinitum*.

To avoid terms like "great," "fine" and especially *ordinaire* which they consider subjective, wine publicists in this country prefer to speak of "standard" and "premium" wine. Anything sold by the fifth in corked bottles is deemed "premium" and anything else a "standard" wine. This won't do. Semantics aside, most of our wine production, like everybody else's, is meant for nigh on immediate consumption. This is what most of us drink most of, and if there's reason not to call it *ordinaire* it should only be that not all "standard" wines are of that grade. Some of them, in our considered judgement, are contemptible. There are others beneath contempt.

Such discrimination is always relative, of course, not only to your own taste and experience but also to the other wines available in the same class. European *ordinaire,* on the whole, is far more ordinary than our own and much of what is consumed in Europe would make even our poorest wine taste good by comparison. It is easy to understand why M. Henri Cruse (of the Bordeaux Cruses) could proclaim a few years ago that Gallo Hearty Burgundy was one of the world's best dollar values in wine. He was right: so it was. But it's a sign of the times (which Gallo *frères* have been among the first to recognize) that Americans are now ready for a better basic minimum red than Gallo Hearty Burgundy.

what's ordinary now?

The merest glance at what's going into jugs these days will amply justify this statement. Robert Mondavi, to start with a winery of super-premium status, released the first bulk red and white in its history a few years ago, with a rosé but a step behind. They ranked well above *ordinaire* grade—and price, to be sure—but there they were, and sold they did. A winery of equal stature, Sebastiani, introduced Cabernet Sauvignon and Chardonnay in jugs, competitive in quality with many winery's fifths and priced about $5, and soon reasonably priced jug varietals were the norm. While not quite *ordinare,* they are a boon to bargain-hunting wine lovers.

As we've seen in a previous chapter, the available quantity of our finest grapes will increase dramatically in the immediate future and almost certainly at a rate the American market cannot absorb. Once the market for fine wines is saturated, what happens to the fine wine that's left over? The answer will be found in the jugs of the future. Even more of them will carry names of noble grapes alongside price tags you'd expect to pay for the

jugs to come

humblest generic wine. Even those labelled "Burgundy" or what-have-you will become better and better as higher proportions of the best grapes are blended into them. The jump in quality of our everyday wines has been a long time coming, as the song says, but it will probably be the most lasting result of our on-going wine revolution. In uncharacteristically gracious fashion, the laws of supply and demand assure the wine consumer of good wines for the price of *ordinaire* over the years to come.

the price of
everyday pleasure

Good wine for the price of *ordinaire!* Therein lies the whole object of our quest for everyday drinking wine, and because our choice is limited to those wines that will not violate our budget, Mr. Belloc's "ordinary wine" category probably summons forth from us more real connoisseurship than all our enjoying of his "special wines." Simply start with the cheapest jugs available and work your way up to the ones that perfectly suit your palate and your purse . . . then keep trying out newly arriving competition. Judge your daily wine as you might a steady lover—if you can be faithful for a week and not lose interest, you're definitely on to something. Personal preference is your only guide.

generically speaking

Most of the contenders will be generic wines, a classification that's easily explained. Whereas present law specifies a minimal 51 percent of a grape variety in any wine bearing that "varietal" name, a generic is always a blend; it can consist of any combination of grape varieties and bears a "European" wine name. Burgundy, Claret and Chianti are the most popular for reds; Chablis, Sauterne and Rhine wine the most common whites.

Now no two wineries have identical recipes for their Chablis, say, or Burgundy, although virtually all of them market a wine of some sort under these names. As you might expect, therefore, the same generic names apply to wines that range from dreadful to just short of fine—even beyond, on rare occasions. No one expects all Irish potatoes to come from Ireland or wants Wisconsin to stop producing Swiss cheese, but wine experts have long maintained that the only *true* Burgundy must come from the region of that name in France and so on down the line. This purism—if you consider it such—is not really unfounded. Environment is infinitely more important than heredity in determining the character of the wine Burgundy's great black grape Pinot Noir, for example, will produce. Furthermore, practically no Pinot Noir is included in the blend for any American-made "Burgundy."

As defined under our law a generic name is meaningless and our generic wines have next to nothing in common with their "originals." "Sauterne" is not so-called because of any imagined similarity to its name-sake but only because the public buys the name. Too often in the past there has been no flavor difference whatever between the Sauterne and Chablis or Burgundy and Claret a given winery produced: They just changed the labels and maybe used a different-shaped bottle. Generic wines comprise far the greatest part of our *ordinaire* and this brings us back to Ernest and Julio.

name-dropping

If we claim their wines taste like God's afterthought, it is not with libelous intent or any desire to affect the success of the world's largest winery, which theirs, by a long shot, is. For this very reason, however, it is also impossible to ignore the Gallos and their chief competitors. It's been estimated that United Vintners (Inglenook, Italian Swiss Colony, Petri, *et al.*) and Gallo between them are responsible for almost 70 percent of California's total wine production. A book like this one should not pass over the largest winery in the land without comment but, on the other hand, a serious rating of their wines is out of the question—they just will not bear that much analysis.

le club Gallo

We regret to report the same holds generally true for their run-of-

the-assembly line relatives from Italian Swiss Colony, Franzia Brothers, Guild-Roma and Carlo Rossi's Red Mountain. We might point out that Ernest and Julio's newest batch of varietals are not assembly-line wines, but bottle for bottle the best mass-market wine we know is Perelli-Minetti, a California Wine Association label. One is compelled to salute all these firms for their historic role in putting wine on the greatest number of dinner tables. In contrast to an unhealthy percentage of European *ordinaire,* their wines are drinkable, after all, and will serve on any occasion when a wine's presence and wetness are more important than its taste.

the best in bulk

California's list of nationally distributed bulk wines has become one of the fastest changing and most competitive arenas in the industry. Quality-wise, it was long dominated by firms like Almadén, Christian Brothers, Inglenook, Louis Martini, C. Mondavi & Sons, etc. Though usually drier, their wines were sometimes no better than their larger competitors, and despite their higher prices you did not always get what you paid for—an *ordinaire*-plus. With most honorable exceptions like Cresta Blanca and San Martin Burgundy, the general quality was probably typified by C. Mondavi & Sons' "CK" brand. "CK" Zinfandel has fallen off noticeably of late and perhaps only their Chablis and "Barberone" (Italian for "big Barbera") represent the good wine we're after. Louis Martini's Mountain Red is very tart and very good indeed; his Mountain White we've found less dependable but still better than *ordinaire.* Both, you should be aware, are about the driest you'll find in jugs. Inglenook diffuses its image considerably by attaching its name to the different "Navalle" and "Inglenook Vintage" grades of jug wine. Their Petite Sirah is the "Vintage" we reach for and consider the only one that seems worth the dollar and a half extra per magnum, a bottle containing the merest fraction less than 51 ounces.

jug juggling

57

These best-known brands will increasingly have to lower their prices and many will need to improve to stay in the running with their new competition, which proliferates with something approaching abandon these days. The rising level of sophistication amongst us American consumers bodes no good for $6.50 per three-liter *ordinaires* like Almadén and Paul Masson. Foppiano and Parducci are producing vintage-dated varietal whites in jugs, as fresh and clean as new snow, while Souverain, a relative newcomer, has entered the lists with both reds and whites of note and carrying birthdates. Robert Mondavi's generics are now bearing vintages, too. Among the notable non-vintaged varietals in jugs, Sonoma Vineyards' Ruby Cabernet, Zinfandel and French Colombard are just fine, while Giumarra's jug Cabernet Sauvignon and Chardonnay are not far behind. Almadén, not to be outdone, is moving toward varietals in jugs, with some vintage dates and some appellations of origin, and they are more than a step in the right direction. Sebastiani, which after all started this whole delightful business, now offers five varietals, the best of which are red—Cabernet, Pinot Noir (a light one) and Zinfandel. Another good Zinfandel, just a shade smoother than the Sebastiani, comes from Foppiano.

recent arrivals

Now by "good" we mean a wine you're surprised to be pouring from a jug. Many of these brands we've mentioned are noteworthy for having pioneered the so-called "valley" or "mid-varietals," predominately Zinfandels, Ruby Cabernets, French Colombards and Chenin Blancs that are grown in the San Joaquin and Central valleys. We're destined to hear a good deal more about them. As a whole they rank considerably above *ordinaire*-grade generics, and seldom exceed them in price. Like most generics, however, they're noticeably less than bone-dry so far.

mid-varietals

In California proper, very few generics sold by the fifth are worth their price, which is to say, cannot be equalled by a good bulk wine. Among those few is Mirassou's 1976 Burgundy, with all the fruitiness and charm of the best Moulin-a-Vent Beaujolais. The BV Burgundy is consistently as distinctive but its peers are hard to find: Heitz Cellars', for instance, or one-shot triumphs such as Charles Krug's 1974 Vintage Selection or Sebastiani's aged and astonishing 1968. Yes, one can carefully choose a fifth of any of these over another winery's jugs at the same price, judgements we have tested in various places and on various incomes.

As we have thus become almost wholly serious about our subject, this must be the time to recall the human dimension of wine buying, as most wine lovers who do not live in California know it. Suppose two fifths, for example, is the average daily intake of one's family and that one winters, as we have, on the Gulf Coast of Mississippi. Most wines available there are, to put it politely, insults to mediocrity. It costs around $50 a week to provide oneself with nothing more than the "good" wine we're talking about. The experience proves Christian Brothers' Burgundy, for example—"the normal excellence" as poet Jack Gilbert might call it—is worth every penny of its price. But you realize likewise that in California an equal amount of wine at least as good need cost just half as much and you could be spending the difference on two or three superlative bottles each week.

the budget bared

California's most unbeatable wine bargains, alas, are doomed to be known only by hearsay outside of the state but some just may represent the wine wave of the future—everyday division—to be distributed for sale in your locale. The most recent one to surprise us utterly was Fetzer's Mendocino Premium Red, but you're likelier to locate a jug of Barengo, Geyser Peak or Parducci. There's Cambiaso, Emile's, Fortino, San Martin and Setrakian; also Gemello, LaMont, the redoubtable Cresta Blanca and Valley of the Moon.

wine bargains

Truly outstanding jug whites are specially hard to find but we regularly swear by Emile's and desert it only for Carbone's Napa DeLuxe White (*sic*—honestly) or Hecker Pass Winery's Chablis. Pedroncelli and Pellegrini also have some claims on our affection, but our list could then go on and on without practical value even to our fellow Californians, whose prejudices in these matters are fully as unreasoning as our own. Most of these wineries have yet to achieve significant distribution across state lines, but all of them reward discovery and fully deserve our chronicling them here.

There is more to life than Burgundy and Chablis but there is one factor besides our taste dictating what we drink and that is money. Offering the best for the money is the whole key to success in the ordinary, everyday wine market—or should be—and we have tried here to describe the best we know in hopes it may amuse some and, if all goes well, be profitable to others. Several facts and other semi-certainties, however, are likely to alter the picture we've drawn beyond recognition before this decade is out. The price per ton of California Cabernet Sauvignon tumbled from $1200 in 1972 to $685 in 1974. In 1975 California vintners could have produced a conservative thirty million more gallons of wine if only they'd had tanks and barrels to hold it all. In the last few years, white wines have become a fad that seemingly will not cease—it is no longer the "cocktail" hour or party, but white-wine time. Supply and demand being different animals, that means a surplus of red wines, and that means bargains.

bright side of the dismal science

In providing this snapshot of the present situation we've given as much guidance as we feel a book honestly can give. No vintner is able to bottle, month in and out, exactly the same wine under each of his labels. The most important thing, from the consumer's standpoint, is that the revolution in quality where our "standard" wines are concerned has just gotten under way. Inevitably, according to enologist Harold Berg of UC Davis, ". . . the average quality of California wines will be so superior that there will be no comparison in the rest of the world." Meanwhile the rest of winedom also furnishes plenty of wines cheap enough for everyday drinking and we do not ignore them in shopping. Our fondly remembered 1968 Campeador Rioja is one of many discoveries worth several times their price, but we will leave them for other books to extol. California wine is today more than ever worth a book to itself.

making it better

Today's rapid up-grading of quality makes any guide to California wines suspect and when we come to fine wines, which in due course we shall, there are particular reasons for viewing with suspicion any volume full of extensive rankings and laborious comparisons. Of necessity such a book is more of an historical document than a consumer's guide by the time it is distributed for sale because so much of the wine considered will already have been sold. The ones remaining will also have been changing constantly, some a little, some a lot, with age.

Finally, and most important, there can almost by definition be no objectivity in matters of taste. The same thing will taste different to the same person depending on whether he's fed or famished, tired or fresh, and so on. Experience and sensitivities vary from person to person also, producing different and equally valid judgements of the same characteristic in a wine of any complexity. A wine we pronounce "robust" may seem to have only medium body to you. The only way to come to know wine, and your own taste in wine, is to drink it.

the purely personal

This is not to say there's no need to seek wise guidance sometimes, and with wine at least the place to look for it is the right wine shop. It won't be the one with a display of wines in the window. If the merchant doesn't know that wines require protection from sunlight and heat, he isn't likely to know too much else about them. The importance of finding a good wine dealer can hardly be overestimated, for he (and not a writer) is the first and indispensable tutor in the buying of special wines. If you're lucky you may find several local shops where you can make purchases and get advice, but by all means choose dealers who drink wine themselves. They are always eager to pass on to you the love of wine they have acquired, and to share with you their many experiences, discoveries and surprises. If a dealer does not take evident pride in his profession and pleasure in discussing with you any wine, its virtues and limitations, before you buy it, he's not the man for you to patronize. Needless to add, no good wine dealer pushes a wine merely because it's expensive or uses snob appeal to try to make a sale.

you & your dealer

A good dealer will tell you that the comparative value of different wines increases out of all proportion to prices. The cost of the bottle, shipping charges, taxes and so forth are the same for a fifth of *ordinaire* as for a fifth of something fine. A wine costing two dollars might be much more than twice as good as a bottle selling for one, therefore, because all the extra goes entirely into the wine. This does not mean that you always get what you pay for, only that a wine that is too cheap is a wine that's too expensive. Fine wines cost dearly because there is never enough for everybody, the demand always exceeds the supply. Only considerable experience or sound advice can procure you the best bargain for your money every time you buy them.

value vs. cost

The best way you can explore the world of fine wines confidently is to find a wine merchant whom you can trust completely to serve as advisor and guide. Besides, half the joy of wine comes from sharing your discoveries with an understanding and sympathetic friend and finding that you can hold your own in the many arguments that arise among wine lovers. It also helps to be able to read a wine label.

One could almost suspect the world's wine producers of conspiring to confuse the consumer with the sonorous words they use on their labels. In most cases there is literally no way the uninitiated can judge from its label how a bottle's contents will taste.

Both Federal and California law control what a wine label may and must not say; and confusing as they are, the California regulations on labelling furnish far more information as to flavor than any others in the world. Champagnes, for example, may be labelled "dry," *"sec,"* *"brut,"* *"nature,"* *"doux,"* or "extra dry." Each of these terms, used to designate degrees of sweetness, is carefully defined only in California's law. California's regulations likewise distinguish among the phrases "produced and bottled," "made and bottled," "estate-bottled," and so forth. "Produced" means at least 75 percent of the wine in the bottle was crushed, fermented and matured by the vintner named. "Made" indicates the vintner was similarly responsible for less than 75 but a minimum of 10 percent of the wine thus labelled. "Bottled at the winery" is another phrase whose use is restricted but which means much the same as "produced." At the exclusive end of the spectrum is the legend "estate-bottled." This appears only when 100 percent of the grapes used were grown on that vineyard and every drop of the wine made in that winery. More recent rulings allow the grapes to be grown any old where at all as long as the land is owned or leased by the vintner. This legal dilution of the meaning of "estate-bottled" has not affected a number of producers like Concannon who still use only those grapes grown adjacent to their wineries for "estate-bottled" wines. "Cellared," "perfected" or "prepared and bottled by" are also sometimes met with, and all mean only

California wine labels

"produced" or "made?"

63

that the bottler put some finishing touches on the wine before calling it his. To satisfy the minimum Federal requirement a label must somewhere state "bottled by" with the bottler's name and place of business.

The words "table wine" or "light wine" sometimes appear in the place of a statement of alcohol contents. Table wines, under California law, must be 10-to 14-percent alcohol, with a tolerance of 1-1/2 percent allowed. A statement of alcohol content is mandatory on all dessert wines, where the legal maximum is 21 percent alcohol and the tolerance only 1 percent.

alcoholic content

All the wine in bottles labelled "California" must be from grapes grown in the state. More specific designation, like "Livermore," "Sonoma," and so forth is allowed when at least 75 percent of the grapes used came from and were fermented in the place named. These requirements can be contrasted with those of other states like New York, which allows up to 25 percent of the grapes used in "New York" wines to be imported from elsewhere. And despite the admirable *"appellation contrôlée"* laws which apply to the more notable French wines, France is still the world's leading importer of wines in bulk for blending with its own production. As one expert has observed, the French are better at writing strict laws than they are at enforcing them.

Bordeaux's much publicized "Winegate" scandal was but one of approximately 250 violations of French wine laws prosecuted that year. In addition, European winemakers for generations have disputed the legal definitions of their district names and these arguments have just begun in California. Before long, knowledgeable wine buyers will be able to specify not simply "California" or "Sonoma" Zinfandel, but one from a specific part of Sonoma, say, or Mendocino. A wine's home address tells a great deal about it and this is as true of Californian wines as of any others. Our Wine

a wine's home address

History chapter reviews this growing movement toward appellations of origin in detail. As in Europe, the more specific the statement of geographical origin on a California label—not Sonoma, for instance, but Alexander Valley—the likelier you are to find it a wine worth remembering.

California law is not nearly so strict when it comes to the actual names of wines, the most mysterious of all the words on the label. We have

varietal labelling

already noted that generic or type-named wines can be made from any and every grape. Most of the "premium" wines are given varietal names, the names of the grape variety from which they are made. Although most of our grapes are of European origin, the names of the different varieties are virtually unknown to the European public. Cabernet Sauvignon and Pinot Noir are familiar to millions of Americans, while Frenchmen who have been drinking the juice of these grapes all their lives will rarely have heard of them. In California as long as a minimum 51 percent of the wine comes from the grape named it is eligible for varietal labelling. True, the 49 percent must always play a silent-partner role so that the wine has the predominant characteristics of the variety designated, but the requirement is still ridiculously low. The wine industry in California has finally seen the light, and recent new regulations state that the varietal minimum shall be raised to 75

the label laws

percent as of January 1, 1983, a time chosen to allow wineries to rearrange their vineyard priorities. Other aspects of the regulations were tightened also, but some avid consumers, disappointed, have gone to court to squeeze some more juice out of the law and the wineries. Where it will end, deponent knoweth not, but it seems certain that the minimums will be raised, at least, and that will be a good thing. I hope the Law will not be an Ass about it; many varietals need blending to smooth and enhance the character of the main ingredient. Some, such as Barbera, need a firm reining-in.

Now for a bit of Bacchic blasphemy on this matter of the vintage date! Vintage years are of very real importance in Europe. Years of bad weather, and thus of poorer wines, recur with such unpleasant frequency there that wine lovers are forced to learn which are the good years simply to avoid buying the bad ones. There's an average annual variation of something like 15 percent in the amount of sunlight suffusing California's vineyards, however, with the result that there simply are no spectacular differences between years in California wines. This does not mean that there are *no* differences, of course. The years 1962 and 1972 were considered less than satisfactory, and 1964, 1968, 1970 and 1974 extraordinary. Wineries always differ in their success with a year's vintage anyway, and even in those years when most wine is fine, poor wine is also produced.

the vintage year

Vintage dates can be used on California wines only when all the grapes used in that wine were harvested and fermented in that year. Wine-makers who do not vintage date their varietals often talk of the need for freshening older wine by blending some younger with it or say they want their wines to have the same flavor every year. With notable exceptions such as the good Christian Brothers, most of them probably want to avoid the problem of selling wines from reputedly poorer years and the requirement of using 75 percent of the designated variety in vintage-dated varietal wines. Every batch of wine will differ somewhat from every other, even in places where "every year's a vintage year," and blending does not produce unchanging aroma and flavor in wines from month to month, much less from year to year. Fortunately, more and more wineries are acknowledging this and using vintage dates. This not only makes it easier for us consumers to find other bottles of some particularly memorable nectar, but it also permits more

vintage dating

intelligent comparisons between the same wines from different wineries. Vintages from the same district occasionally display an overall style as easily identifiable as Edward Gibbons' or El Greco's. Most important, the vintage date tells the wine's birthday.

a matter of age

Any discussion of vintage dates calls for a digression on the related subject of aging. Most of the world's wines are consumed before they are even a year old for the very good reason that they would get no better if they were stored longer. Unfortunately, very few of the California wines which do profit from bottle aging are allowed time to mature. Beginning in 1970, the government finally stopped taxing vintners and merchants on their entire warehouse inventory every year, which had made the proper aging of certain wines on their premises prohibitively costly. Not all fine wines require aging, of course. Each has its own time for reaching maturity,

peaking/fading

staying at its peak, and then beginning to fade. Whites, on the whole, will have attained their optimum fragrance and flavor within a year or so of vintage, though some people prefer them at three or four years. Rosés are often best at about six months. Red wine generally needs more time to reach its best, but this varies. Some Cabernet Sauvignon may well be undrinkable until it has passed the five-year mark and may continue to improve for decades thereafter, while most Beaujolais or Red Pinot is usually long past its prime at the end of a decade. Zinfandel may be drunk as young or as old as you like. "Old wine, like old friends, the best," is thus a blanket inaccuracy, even if some poet did say it. Age is *not* the noblest of all vinous virtues; except in the case of certain fine and long-lived reds, age is deceptive as an indication of quality. If you want to know how old a wine without a vintage date is, try looking at the bottom of the bottle. Most manufacturers of American wine bottles blow into the bases of their bottles a record of the year in which they were made, usually two digits next to the hallmark ('68, '69, '70). Figuring that the better wineries keep their reds in the wood for at least two years before bottling, the whites one year, and the rosés under a year, you can determine the age of the wine fairly accurately.

To return now to our labels. You frequently find on them strange numbers or words like "private stock," "private reserve" or "limited bottling." None of these terms is regulated by law; they can indicate higher quality wines, or they can be entirely without meaning and intended only to impress. Cask, *cuvée* and bin numbers are the most mystifying because no explanation of their deeper meanings is ever found on the labels that carry them. They just conceivably may help you identify wine from some particular batch that you liked so that you can get more of the same. Anyway, they look impressive. Your only guide as to whether or not to ignore all such notations as these must be the reputation of the individual wineries involved and, of course, the good advice of your wine dealer. Our glossary should be useful in unravelling the intricacies of foreign wine labels, but you must also look to the good offices of your wine merchant for aid. If he's worthy of your trust, you may learn a great deal from him about the judicious selection of wine. Someone you may *not* trust nine times out of ten is the *sommelier,* wine steward or wine waiter from whom you order your wine in a restaurant. Rest assured the restaurant will make a very handsome profit on whatever wine you order there; most charge at least 100 percent more than a liquor store would for the same bottle. The less likely its clientele is to be familiar with a given wine, the more likely the restaurant is to charge even more for it. In too many places part of the sommelier's job is simply to sell its highest-priced vintages. On the other hand, the least expensive wines are usually the ones with the highest markups. The best buys on the wine list

the indecipherable

you and
your wine steward

generally lie somewhere between these extremes. Unless you know the restaurant, trusting to the selection of a waiter may procure you no more than an expensive name and not necessarily an appropriate wine.

restaurant wines

The conditions in which wine is kept in restaurants and the handling it receives are with few exceptions far from ideal. Unless you can afford (at their prices) to risk a disappointing bottle, it's a good idea to order the finest wines only when you know all about the restaurant and have good reason to trust it. The best wines, such as better restaurants pride themselves on stocking, cannot be whisked to your table in a state ready for immediate consumption. After all, it has been imprisoned in its bottle perhaps ten years awaiting your summons, and deserves a chance to take the air, to stretch and expand, before it can possibly be expected to put on its best

performance. It's criminal not to allow a very fine or great wine half an hour, say, between the time it's uncorked and the time you drink it. In fact, all red wines should profit from being allowed such a breathing space so that the bouquet can really blossom and show off. You'll have to arrange this with the waiter since it is unfortunately not common practice in this country.

giving it air

It's too much to ask of any wine that it go well with any wide gastronomic variety. If there's no unanimity about the food your party wants, neither can there be any about the wine. If you are all determined to drink the same wine together, there's always Champagne or rosé. These may represent the easiest choice, but in our opinion they are rather a poor compromise. There's always that certain wine we think would set off some dish to perfection, and it seems a pity to do without it. The only solution then is to order more than one kind of wine, either a one-tenth bottle for each person or a whole bottle of both red and white. White wines need no time to breathe, but it's a good idea to have them arrive at the table early also. If the wine has been in a bin somewhere, it will need some little while in an ice bucket to cool. If it's just come from a refrigerator, it may well be too cold and need time to warm.

more than one

In due course the wine steward returns with your selection(s) and goes into his act with the corkscrew, first showing you the label so you know you are getting what you ordered. If he doesn't offer you the cork, ask to see it. Look at it. If the bottom is wine soaked then the wine has been stored properly on its side. Smell it. If it smells like cork—and not like wine—the wine is almost surely corky. If the sommelier is especially pretentious, you may want to bite the bloody cork just to watch his reaction. Then he will pour a half-inch into your glass and await your judgement. The first thing to look out for is corkiness, an uncommon but unmistakable disorder, a fierce

the opening act

when to send wine back

mustiness that assaults nose and palate immediately. Many a good bottle has other funny smells immediately upon opening, so if you're not pleased with your first sniff, swirl the wine for a while and see if the odor goes away. Whites may be tainted with sulphur, and reds sometimes have something mildewy about them. If these smells persist and are confirmed by the taste, you've got a bad bottle and should send it back. Any restaurant will take back bottles so afflicted. If it's been stored too long in a place too hot for it, the wine will taste dead and despondent and should also be sent back.

and whether

Sending back wine which has no gross defects but simply is not up to expectations depends, we suppose, on how sure you are of what that wine ought to be. Few restaurants will risk alienating business by starting an argument over the matter if you look as though no discussion is going to change your mind. Remember that you're not bound to accept what's offered you, in any case, and it's a shame to accompany a really good meal with a less-than-satisfactory wine.

the home supply

Cellars are liquid libraries. Young wines need a kind master and a good home in which to reach maturity. If you do have a basement or garage, or even closet space which is dark, dry and above all, cool and constant in temperature, get yourself some plywood and construct a few diamond-shaped bins. By dovetailing the bottlenecks, we've been able to get dozens and dozens of bottles into a single bin, two feet by two feet and eighteen inches deep. A number of these enable you to retrieve the bottle you want without disturbing your whole cache. Thus prepared, you may buy your wines young and drink them old. Most fine reds are sold long before they are ready to drink, and the price of the small amount remaining skyrockets as the wine improves. Moreover, you can almost always get a 10-percent discount buying wines by the case.

Refine thy raptures. If thou drink, drink by the eight and ninety rules of art: if thou love, exceed by delicacy.

—Aleister Crowley

erving wine requires nothing more than a corkscrew and some glassware. Both deserve some comment. The ideal corkscrew exists only in heaven. The wide variety of corkscrews existing on earth all have something wrong with them. Many are exasperating and some are dangerous. With most you must put the bottle between your knees, holding it with the left hand and fighting the often reluctant cork with your right. This method can rupture the puller and, if he has a weak heart, kill him stone dead. This perilous waste of effort often accomplishes nothing anyway. A better sort of corkscrew does all the work mechanically, either by means of levers or else with a fancy reverse-action screw on top which lifts the cork out as if it were pulled by a giant. These are generally much more satisfactory than the first *earthly* kind, but they also have their deficiencies. The lever-principle ones lead *corkscrews* rather sooner than later to scraped knuckles. The reverse-action, lift-out types usually either have worms with cutting edges or worms that are not long enough for all corks. Thus even when you're able to get the worm in, you run the risk of tearing the center out of an old cork with all that added mechanical power.

Our favored implement at the moment of writing is an ingenious item of Danish design which is not, in fact, a corkscrew at all. It consists of a wooden handle with two flat and tapering metal fangs attached and requires a very patient operator in order to work. You insert the flat metal pieces on either side of the cork and gradually work them down between it and the neck of the bottle. By alternating pressure from side to side very cautiously, you finally get the metal pieces past the cork, then twisting this way and that you draw it out easy as pie. It may or may not be helpful to know that

the German name for this instrument is pronounced "ah-so," but more than that we do not know ourselves. Patiently applied, it works very well for us most of the time. It doesn't work at all when the bottle neck slopes away from the cork a few deceptive fractions of an inch inside the lip of the bottle. We've discovered that bottles thus fiendishly engineered come mainly from Germany and Argentina.

the heavenly corkscrew

From the foregoing it should be obvious that we may as well resign ourselves to the utter depravity of inanimate objects. Still, it is helpful to envision the characteristics of the heavenly corkscrew while we are shopping for yet another one to try out. It has, to begin with, a worm long enough to transfix even the longest cork. The point is not dead center, but rather exactly in line with its spirals. These are without cutting edges, and there's an open space down the center. And lastly, we are confident the good God has contrived a mechanism which eliminates tugging and muttered curses. But until this device is bequeathed us mortals, we can only go on looking for the corkscrew that combines most of these attributes in itself.

glassware

If the simple matter of the best corkscrew is complicated, the complicated question of the "right" glassware is simple. Manufacturers, advertisers and salesmen of glassware would all have us believe that Burgundy and Claret, Rhine and Moselle, are each properly served only in its own distinctively shaped glass. They convinced our grandmothers this was the case, and bars and restaurants reinforce these old-fashioned affectations today. There is even a "proper" glass for serving rosé d'Anjou! All this has made for good business ever since Victorian days, but it's played hell with good sense. A squadron of wineglasses beside every place setting may be a pretty sight, but they make no difference to the taste of the wine that's served in them and this is what really counts. Only people hopelessly brainwashed by crystal salesmen and Madison Avenue can still pretend there are such creatures as "proper" glasses for different wines. ("And this is the Chianti glass in our new Corinthian candle pattern, Madam.") The truth of the matter is a glass that's good for any wine is a good glass for every wine.

Good wineglasses show off the wine; therefore they are not tinted or ornamented in any way that distorts the wine's color. A good wineglass is large enough to hold half a pint, or almost. This way when half full it holds a reasonable amount and still leaves plenty of room at the top for the bouquet to collect. So that you can get bouquet and taste all at once, there should be room for your nose inside the rim when you tip your glass to drink from it. And so that you can swirl the wine to your heart's content and not lose any of its perfumes, a good wineglass has to be tulip shaped. The ideal wineglass, in short, is any big, clear, tulip-shaped piece of stemware that's not too costly to replace nor so fragile as to require replacement often.

the ideal glass

But what of Champagne, Sherry and brandy glasses you ask? A few concessions, but no quarter. Unless you're a glassware hobbyist, that Victorian trinket, the Sherry glass, should hold no more charm for you than it will Sherry. The largest, filled brimful won't hold a decent-sized drink. They are easily spilled. In Spain, Sherry's native land, it is always served in glasses like our all-purpose, tulip-shaped stemware.

It's no compliment to Helen of Troy that some wag supposed our latter-day Champagne glasses were modelled on her breasts. Actually, of course, these glasses date from the same period that gave us the tuxedo and a host of similar social "refinements." Sparkling wines have scent like any other, but both scent and effervescence are only wasted in Champagne glasses. Try to smell the bouquet and you just get bubbles in your nose; you'd be better off drinking your Champagne out of slippers. The oldest

Champagne glasses

Champagne glasses we've ever seen were of pressed glass and made in Waterford, Ireland, around 1780. They were frosted to conceal the sediment champagne makers had not yet discovered how to eliminate and shaped like regular wineglasses more or less but had hollow stems. Hollow-stemmed glasses show off the effervescence to advantage and retain it longer, but special glasses are not really necessary for Champagne—the all-purpose glassware we've described serves admirably. Just by all means avoid that saucer-on-a-stem called a Champagne glass.

The all-purpose glass is also perfectly adequate for brandy, though you may find the traditional brandy-snifter shape with its shorter stem easier to handle. The idea is to stimulate the volatile fumes by warming the brandy with the palm of your hand; the thinner the glass is, therefore, the headier your brandy's bouquet.

If you do happen to own a cabinet full of glassware, you'll want to use your largest for Burgundies, your slightly smaller, narrower glasses for white and/or Bordeaux-type red wines, and the ones with the longest stems for the various Alsatian and Rhine-type wines. On the other hand, if you do not happen to own such a variety of glasses, there's really no necessity for acquiring them. Of course it is convenient to have enough glasses of some sort to serve two or more wines at a meal without having to wash up between courses.

sediment

A corkscrew and glasses of some sort are all the special equipment you need to enjoy wine. But there are a few things to consider before you raise the first glass to your lips. An old red wine may have thrown a sediment during its years in the bottle. This is only natural, and in most cases the taste of the wine would be unaffected even if you drank all the dregs off. Being frankly lazy, we prefer just to handle such bottles gently and pour carefully and manage to avoid getting much sediment in any but the last glass or two.

If you're unhappy at the thought of drinking sediment or want your wine to be perfectly brilliant in the glass, decanting is the only answer. Take care not to stir up the sediment while handling and opening the bottle; then gently pour the wine from its original bottle into a decanter in front of a white surface or a light. When the light reveals tiny specks swimming past, it's time to stop pouring. Decanting is something you'll rarely need to bother with, but whenever possible you will want to open your red wines an hour or more before drinking them. Some people do this with white wines too. It certainly doesn't hurt them, but it's never seemed to improve white nearly as much as red wine. This chance to take the air makes the wine much livelier and more fragrant. Try it sometime with two bottles of the same wine, opening one an hour beforehand and the other immediately before drinking. You'll be amazed at the difference and begin to think, as we do, that you're not really getting the full pleasure when the wine you drink hasn't been allowed time to breathe.

giving
wine breathing space

There's also the question of Fahrenheit and centigrade to consider before you get around to drinking your wine. Rosés and whites, it's generally agreed, are better chilled and reds somewhat below normal room temperature. But to some people chilled means icy and to others barely cool. You'll find if wine is very cold it doesn't have much smell to it (which explains all those labels instructing "serve very well chilled"). Some people make much of the "ideal" temperature for this white or that—too much, actually, for the wine is mouth temperature soon after it passes our lips. It's up to you— there's no such thing as a right temperature. Lots of people also refrigerate their Sherry and Port. Adjusting wine's temperature and letting it breathe are not mandatory, but wine—as the wise old ancients knew—is in reality a god

temperature

and will pay you back with added pleasure for every premeditated courtesy you show it.

A liter of wine contains an eighth of a man's nourishment and nine-tenths of his good humor, as some anonymous authority has noted truthfully. Nobody ever heard of a man enjoying a good wine and going out to assassinate another. And it's demonstrably nourishing. Wine's greatest contribution to the betterment of mind and body, however, comes from the power it possesses to complement the finest food and compensate for the poorest. Pray take note, however: There are some few foods and condiments *known no-no's* with which any wine tastes terrible and which will taste terrible with wine. Our unpleasant experiences over a number of years have produced this rather Rabelaisian list: anchovies, candied yams, citrus fruits, all pickles, smoked herring, bananas, Boston baked beans, curries, chocolates, horseradish, molasses, and Worcestershire, mint and Tabasco sauces. Also mustard, and especially vinegar. Vinegar is probably wine's worst enemy. (M. de Caso's culinary genius, thankfully, has devised a final solution to the salad problem: hearts of lettuce with salt and pepper, olive oil and dry-wine dressing. Wines will go with this and this goes with wines!) There are, no doubt, other dishes and sauces which spoil wine as completely as all of the above, but these are the known offenders to date. Beware!

As for what goes with what, the title of this chapter, you're really on your own. "Red wine with red meats, white with white, anything with *out-of-fashion* rosé!" is not inscribed somewhere on a tablet of stone. Such rules are made *tastes* to be broken, if not ignored. Brillat-Savarin, that greatest of French gourmandisers and author of *The Physiology of Taste,* has nothing whatever to say about which wines and foods make the best companions. His contemporary, Napoleon, loved his savory, full-bodied Chambertin Burgundy with practically everything he ate. Even the epicures of the late nineteenth century would flabbergast a present-day wine steward with their ideas of the right wine to accompany the various courses of a formal dinner. The idea of ending a meal with shrimp canapés and a very sweet Sherry might induce convulsions today, but it was once done. The wine lover is an ultraconservative creature, and it takes a lot to induce him to give up his old habits for something new, however good it may be. But however slowly, habits and taste do change, and the best taste teaches us we need not indenture ourselves to the prejudices prevailing in our own times. We're fully entitled to our own eccentricities and should encourage others in theirs.

aperitifs

The most that can be said for the combinations of wine and food that follow is that we like them. There are, of course, any number of wines people drink as aperitifs before the food appears. This seems to us the best of all the many uses to which dry Champagne can be put. Sweet drinks often tend to depress rather than stimulate the appetite, but this depends upon the individual and there's no need to avoid sweet aperitifs. If you haven't already, you should consider the bitter ones. We personally would choose a Campari on ice over any Sherry or Vermouth, sweet or dry. Sherry does go wonderfully well with clear soups—goes well in them too, and Marsala perhaps even better. A preliminary glass of whatever wine you're having with the meal makes an excellent appetizer-drink too, especially when you're having something white and chilled.

alliances with reds

Except for certain soufflés, egg dishes are treacherous. Many don't get along well with wine—fine wine at least. Young Zinfandel or Chianti have no nuances to lose and will stand up to an omelette very nicely. For the same reason, Chianti or Barbera are the obvious choices to go with spicy pastas like lasagna and spaghetti. Choice cuts of red-blooded meat which is not so highly seasoned as to overpower the finesse of a fine wine will admirably accompany the finest you can put beside it. There are many very good, unpretentious wines like Sicily's Corvo which combine well with good, unpretentious items like sausage or liver and bacon. Boeuf Bourguignon provides an excellent excuse for a bottle of the best French Burgundy you can find. Some prefer lighter wines such as Pinot St. George with lamb but Cabernet Sauvignon may have been created chiefly in order *lamb* to accompany this divinest of meats. Game always calls for red wines, supposedly, but we found Charles Krug Chenin Blanc and sweeter Rhine types set off the last venison we had as admirably as any red could. A regrettable lack of venison has held up further research. Southern specialties like fried rabbit or baked bobwhite would surely be affronted by white wines though. Cornish game hen, turkey and chicken are neutral dishes, so to *poultry* speak, that can be adapted to go with practically any wine. When prepared with a wine sauce, the chicken is ordinarily best served with that same wine. Roast turkey surely forms one of the best of all possible backgrounds for a great wine—be the wine white or red.

When you come to the meats which are without red blood and strong *white meats* savor, principally pork and veal, it's best to avoid the more forceful red wines. Indeed, we tend to avoid reds altogether with such fare in favor of full-bodied whites which have some suggestion of sweetness: certain Sauvignon Blancs and Rieslings are perfect. A light red or rosé may please you more. There's never been a "traditional" wine to go with ham, apparently. A large minority would match it with a Claret perhaps, but a dry rosé would be the choice of most people.

The fruit of the sea in all its multitudinous forms is almost always allied with white wines. We say almost, for among other experiments we

fish

have tried hot baked salmon with Château Margaux 1959 and found the combination really excellent. (Salmon usually takes to whites of great character—Meursault, Pouilly-Fuissé, excellent Chardonnays). We also enjoy good red wine with bouillabaisse the same way people in New Orleans do. But these are about the only cases that come to mind where red wines really enhance fishy flavors. We generally find the more acidic white wines tend to offset any sharp fishiness and go best with fish dishes. Oysters, crab meat, shrimp and especially lobster taste splendid indeed with such light, tart wines as Pinot Blanc, Chablis, dry Graves, Pouilly-Fuissé, et cetera, depending on what's available and what you feel like drinking, generally the drier the better. Fish with cream sauces or any strongly flavored fish will take to richer, heavier whites—dry Semillon, Sauvignon Blanc, Chardonnay and company—than will flaky, delicate red snapper, flounder, whitefish and such, when cooked in butter or simply broiled.

With cheeses, red wines are often better than whites, especially when the cheese is strong enough to walk away under its own power. Some of these can smother any wine except maybe heavy old Port. The cream or cottage cheese that often goes along with a soup or chicken salad luncheon seems made for the rosé appropriate to such occasions. Fruits (other than citrus varieties, remember) are also good with white or red, sweet or dry wines. Sweet desserts are often matched with sweet dessert wines, but different sweetnesses often seem to us to battle one another. A glass of Barsac, Muscat de Frontignan or a really luscious Château d'Yquem (three or four glasses!) are by themselves enough to put a perfect finish on a meal.

desserts

There are a few other discoveries we've made. Chinese food, for example, can be even more exotic with, say, Green Hungarian, Chenin Blanc or any such white, semi-sweet "little" wine. Also: if you're eating Mexican

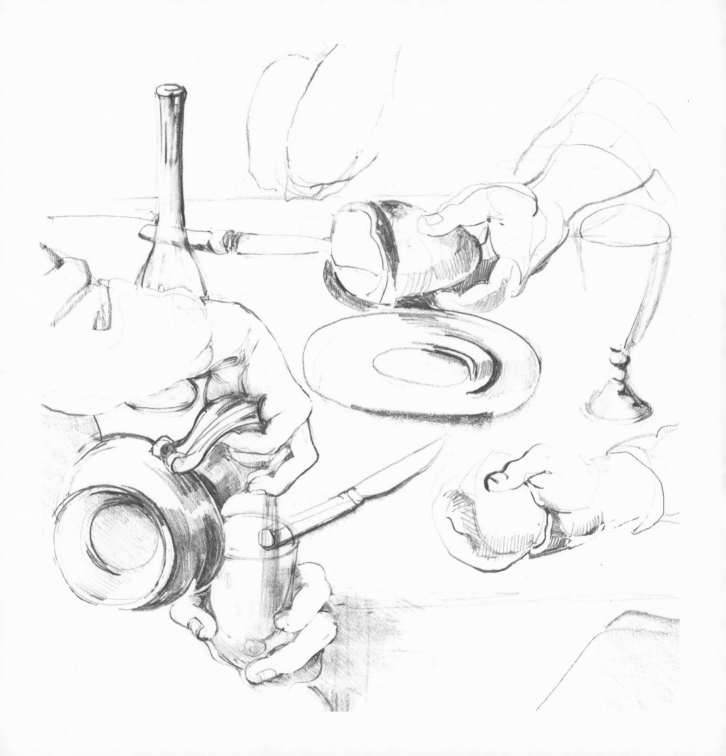

food, drink beer! That's it to date: a rapid and disorderly review of some of our favorite alliances between foods and wines. There are further suggestions listed separately with each wine in the back of the book, to be discarded or disbelieved at will. The idea of "classic harmonies" is not an outright hoax, but the idea is too strait-laced to allow much experimentation and thus can misguide rather than help us discover our individual tastes. The vast majority of the world's wine drinkers, let us not forget, consume the one wine they produce locally with everything they eat, all their lives. They'd laugh at anybody who told them they were wrong.

"classic harmonies"

A gracious little habit to observe in serving wine is to pour an inch or so (less than a full serving) into your own glass first. "Pouring the cork," as it's called, insures that any bits of cork in the wine go into the glass of the host. After serving everybody else you can come back to your own glass and give yourself a full serving. This is customary because it's considerate, not because it looks nice. This brings us to some *sec* and *demi-sec* remarks on matters of so-called ritual. Even today the neo-Emily Postites are engaged in rear-guard action to enforce the most ostentatious ceremonial in serving wine. They deplore the appearance of cocktails before, or cigarettes with wine. They insist the bottle can be brought to the table only if ensconced in a wine cradle or wrapped in a napkin. They have elaborate theories about the order in which guests should be served and the correct wines for each course of a meal.

pomp
and circumstances

Working our way backward through this list, we've already seen that the "correct" wines are the ones we enjoy. Unless you're sufficiently taste blind to serve Champagne with candy, you're in no danger of serving an "incorrect" one. Good manners would dictate that one's guests be served as unobtrusively as possible, so any order that's most convenient would be the one that's most correct. Some people find wire or wicker cradles handy for holding a bottle they intend to decant in one position while they open it; apart from this, the cradle has no function at all. A napkin may prevent a bottle that is wet from chilling in an ice bucket from dripping, but there's no real necessity for using one even then, and it would be purest affectation any other time. Rather than take the edge off your sensitivity, you may want to forego the martini and tobacco when you're expecting to drink a wine such as you are not likely to taste again for six months or a year. If you're drinking a rare wine, something you expect to waft you away with unearthly delight, it would be downright foolish and disrespectful to drink cocktails before the wine appeared or to smoke while it is before you. But then it all depends on you. God knows there's plenty of smoking at the professional winemen's great gourmet banquets in Europe. What the little old ladies of both sexes forget when they formulate rules for serving wine is that wine is primarily for enjoyment, and not for show.

wines in succession

If you're planning to serve different wines with the several courses of a meal, however, you'll find that you enjoy each of the wines more if you figure out beforehand the best order in which to serve them. If menus and memoirs are to be believed, our ancestors could appreciate a succession of five or six fine wines at a sitting. They were made of sterner stuff and that seems a bit excessive today. If you really have occasion to arrange wine serving on such a scale, here are several disasters we now know how to avoid. Foremost is the wine that comes on like gangbusters. A Late Harvest Zinfandel, for instance, or Johannisberg Riesling Spätlese simply chew up the wine that follows. They're so overwhelming there can be no subsequent comparisons: It's time to bring out the brandy and tobacco and be done. If one wine is going to tower over the rest it's best served last anyway, in our view, though not necessarily alongside the high point of the meal. Having more than one genuinely great wine on the menu is the definition of a sumptuous occasion. It's generally true that white wines are more charming and better tasting when drunk before red wines, but this truth is particularly easy to ignore: just plot it. Always select wines you personally have drunk *more than once;* in other words remember above all your fellow diners are not interested in your experimental pursuits, they simply want the wine to taste outstandingly good. Like the gangbuster variety, fortified and sparkling wines will play havoc with your palate when they come *between* still table wines. Let 'em precede or follow only, if you ask us.

white before what?

Serving more than one red or white with a meal provides an opportunity to experiment with all sorts of comparisons and contrasts. You might have different Burgundies of the same vintage, or different vintages of the same Burgundy. You can contrast a fine California Cabernet Sauvignon with a fine French Claret. You may also enjoy very dissimilar wines at the same meal, but in this case it's especially wise for the wines to run in an ascending scale: "little" wines before the "big" ones, and young ones before the old ones, generally speaking. All this comparing is the more interesting when you have friends at hand to disagree with you. Serving more than one wine from time to time will remind you that the differences in vintages or between two wines of the same family are far from imaginary. Comparing one wine with the taste of another is obviously more difficult in memory than when they are served one after the other.

red on red

instant knowledge

To conclude, some words on quantity may be in order. The capacity for wine varies enormously from person to person of course. As an overall average, however, a fifth-sized bottle will serve three or even four people of (very) moderate thirst throughout a typical meal. Naturally, the richer and

more plentiful the food, the more wine you will want and the more you can consume without any noticeable effect. An outright feast may enable all hands to down well over two bottles of wine apiece and risk no loss of composure. But the food had better be very rich indeed and the meal very leisurely should you want to test this statement. One or two glasses of white wine are usually enough to wash down a fish course when you plan to have meat with a red wine afterwards. A half-bottle is plenty for two people, or a whole bottle for three or four in such cases. A bottle of Sherry provides twelve servings of two ounces each, or enough for six people if everyone wants a second glass. If you're having a dry Champagne before dinner, or a sweet Champagne with dessert you can figure on six glasses per bottle.

Finally, don't drink wine if you mean to drug yourself with alcohol. In the first place, you can't really appreciate what you're drinking once you are drunk. In the second place, as Kipling put it

It's no time for mirth and laughter

That cold grey dawn of the morning after.

Overindulgence in wine produces a hangover of memorable and surpassing intensity. The best thing to do about a hangover is to avoid it. This is easily accomplished if at the first signs of inebriation you consume copious droughts of water, which God in His infinite mercy has obviously intended as the antidote to drunkenness. But there are certain sins for which the quality of mercy simply will not be strained, and God offers no antidote for the hangover. The Italians do. It contains every herb from aloes to zedoaria and is the one aperitif you will want to consume in strictest moderation since it can be a remarkably effective laxative if overdone. It's called Fernet-Branca and most people find it vile beyond belief. We admit it's the furthest-out flavor in Christendom, but it helps.

Wine is a living thing. It is made, not only of grapes and yeasts, but of skill and patience. When drinking it remember that to the making of that wine has gone, not only the labor and care of years, but the experience of centuries.

—Allan Sichel

he flavor of wine starts on the vine. "Viticulture," Idwal Jones has observed, "is a profound and ancient art. The simplest of farmers, if it is their calling, may triumph in it; the ablest of scientists may be baffled by it." Raising grapes is year-round work. As soon as one year's vintage is over, the next year's cultivation begins. A grapevine will live fifty or sixty years if allowed its natural span (and many have lasted much longer), but for optimum yield most vineyards in this country replace their *viticulture* vines every thirty-five years or so. New rootstock is set out and in the fall of its first growing season comes time to graft onto it the variety carefully selected for that particular piece of ground. Stakes are driven into place to support each vine; some of the nobler grapes will be trained along wires between the stakes. There is no significant yield for the first four or five years. Then before springtime the vineyard must be pruned.

Man learned grafting and pruning at some midpoint between the time of Noah and Virgil whose Latin verses give directions as precise as only a farmhand's could be, and the work is done by hand today the same as always. "Her vine," the Duke of Burgundy in Shakespeare's *Henry V* laments in time of war, "the merry cheerer of the heart, unprunèd, dies." While it may not die "unprunèd," it certainly loses its vigor and lessens its yield. Skillful pruning determines the arrangement of the next season's fruit on the vine. Finally, the vineyard must be weeded before spring brings the tender new growth and the time of waiting.

Will there be frost, rain, drought, fog? Anxiety over the weather welds wine men to their vineyards. A five-minute hailstorm can wipe out a year's growth. At intervals the vines must be sprayed to ward off blight:

pesticide to prevent leafhoppers, sulphur dust to guard against Oidium fungus. As soon as the leaves are old enough for the rabbits to lose interest in them, they become attractive to the deer. The ripening grapes must be shared with the bees and the birds. Whether it's a good year depends upon the amount of sunshine, but all the influences that affect the quality of the wine cannot be read on the temperature chart. There are other, more mysterious factors too subtle to be recorded. A favorable drift of air, or moonlight, or some inexplicable stir among the bacteria in the soil or in the bloom or fuzz of the grape all have their effect. Tests for sugar and acid are made more and more frequently until finally the vineyard owner decrees it time the harvest begin. The work, gruelling and sweaty, proceeds swiftly.

Scientists will probably never be able to define wine adequately in purest scientific terms. Chemical and other analyses have revealed to date almost four hundred constituent elements in wine and the list, no doubt, will get longer. Despite this accumulation of research, laboratory experiments aimed at producing synthetic wine have never succeeded. It remains the product of grapes and yeast, two forms of plant life which mysteriously bring forth a third living substance—wine. Just as the egg must be fertilized, the grape juice or must requires for its transformation the attack of bacteria. For some reason, so long as the grapes remain on the vine this cannot occur. From the very moment when a bunch of grapes is picked, however, or sometimes even a little bruised, the bacteria begin their work of metamorphosis and the birth of the wine has begun. The winemaker does not really make the wine, therefore, he merely helps nature accomplish her work perfectly. He is thus a kind of obstetrician: he must be professionally competent but also a little inspired and very patient, for the process can last a number of weeks. He adds yeasts to insure victory over the bad ferments

birth of wine

which would turn the developing wine into vinegar. He must keep the fermentation from stopping or getting "stuck" before it has finished. He must guard against a possibly fatal fever. But mainly he can only watch and wait until it is time for him to fill out the official forms, the birth certificate of the new vintage. Virtually all the wines of the Northern hemisphere are born Libra or Scorpio.

The grapes are brought from the fields directly to the crusher which removes the stems. The grape skins, pulp and must go directly into the vats or huge glass-lined tanks. In the case of white wines, the must is first separated from the skins. All grapes have white juice, and either black or white grapes may be used for white wines. The color of wine comes from the inside of the grape skin. Since these pigments are soluble in alcohol, the skins of white wine grapes must be separated from the must before fermentation begins. Rosés are left to ferment on the skins for a short time. Reds are left longer, until the sugar content of the must is between 2 and 8 percent. Then the wine-to-be is pumped into other casks or tanks to complete fermentation. The winemaker regularly takes the temperature of the bubbling and hissing liquid and checks its sugar content. White wines are generally fermented in *closed* containers at temperatures between 50 to 60 degrees Fahrenheit; while reds, in *open* containers while on the skins, ferment at temperatures up to 85 degrees. Once the developing wine has been separated from its "pomace" (pulp, skins, et cetera), it should complete its fermentation without exceeding 70 degrees. If the heat in the vats is not controlled, it may kill off the yeasts and put a premature end to their industrious activity. Chilling the must for a white wine during its fermentation may protract the process to twelve weeks or even longer. This considerably heightens the wine's fruitiness and allows the winemaster to very precisely control the

black grapes
white grapes

balance and degree of dryness. The potential for perfection and for experiment this technology represents is tremendous. Though a recent innovation, cold fermentation has contributed more than any other factor to improving California white wines.

Up until the Second World War the best reds might be left on the skins for two weeks or more. The large amount of tannin imparted by the grape seeds over such a period rendered the new wine harsh, often to the point of undrinkability, until it had been allowed to age in the bottle for a number of years. Nowadays, most winemakers both in California and abroad leave their reds on the skins for an average of four to six days. The wine that results has less tannin and consequently matures earlier. Twenty years ago, for instance, Beaulieu aged their Georges de Latour Reserve Cabernet Sauvignon for eight years before it was marketed, today it is put up for sale after only four years: a difference of four years in the bottle!

When fermentation is finished, the wine receives its first "racking." It is drawn off the lees (sediment in the fermenting vat) into cooperage for aging. White-oak barrels and casks holding from fifty to a thousand gallons allow just enough air to filter through the pores for the wine to breathe a

in the wood little, but not too much. The size and sort of cooperage depend on the wine. Oak or redwood tanks with a capacity of several thousand gallons may be used. Evaporation also occurs while the wine is in the wood, and loss on the order of 8 to 10 percent (including loss from the lees) is not unusual for the first year. Every few weeks therefore each barrel must be "topped up to the bung," that is filled to the barrel hole, to prevent the harm too much air contact would cause. This is called "ullage."

Now the wine has been delivered, but no one can tell what future awaits the newborn, although the winemaker can readily see whether it is plump or thin, healthy or sickly. But if it is born into the nobility, he must await the springtime, when the wine is six months of age, more or less, before he can with some accuracy judge what qualities are latent within it and how the youngster should be reared. The growth and development of a new wine is determined by a series of extremely complex actions and interactions about which almost nothing is known. Like every other form of life, wine needs to breathe, and oxidation is the chief influence in its development. But if it is to develop properly, wine should have less and less oxygen the older it gets. Whites and rosés require less than reds, generally speaking, and some reds need much more than others. How a wine is treated and stored thus depends upon its nature and its age.

a wine is born

American winemakers generally choose to rack their wines less and filter them more often than their European counterparts. Racking is like taking the wine out for a little walk in the fresh air; it not only clarifies but also promotes aging by speeding up oxidation. The lees that are left behind consist mainly of microscopic particles of soil, dead microbes, bits of cream of tartar, flecks of grape skin and suchlike dreck. The ever-attentive wine-master, tasting and analyzing, must also decide when the wine is ready for "fining." On every step in winegrowing and winemaking there are at least two opposing schools of thought, but fining methods defy enumeration. The idea is a sort of reverse filtering whereby the filter passes through the wine instead of vice versa. Gelatin and casein are probably the fining agents most often employed by California wineries, but there are many who swear by more traditional materials like egg white, isinglass, skim milk or beef blood. Whatever is used is spread in a thin veil over the wine and given a number of days or weeks to settle out, collecting on its way to the bottom any infinitesimal particles that may be suspended in the wine. After fining

racking

fining

comes the real filtration(s) and the filters employed are often fine enough to trap microbes.

In a later chapter, we shall consider the trend certain smaller, "boutique" wineries are pioneering to use the lightest possible fining/filtration and even to omit it where possible. If the wine is blended, it is allowed a "marrying" period to see whether it requires additional treatment.

"bottle sickness"

At last the winemaster judges his vintage properly clarified and sufficiently aged for bottling. The wine has come of age. It will not stop developing in its new glass home, but the process will be slower since it must henceforth breathe through a cork. As we have noted elsewhere, the size of the bottle will naturally determine the rate at which bottle aging occurs. The wine is then binned for at least six months until its inevitable "bottle sickness" passes and it has acclimatized itself to its enclosure.

As the public becomes more appreciative or just curious where winemaking's concerned, wine labels in many cases really try to inform. Our glossary is meant to illumine for you the significance of such specifics as you'll find puzzling, Balling or Brix degrees, acidity and so forth. But most wines, let us remember, receive no such upbringing as we have described, and moreover do not deserve it. *Ordinaire* comprises perhaps nine-tenths of the total annual wine production. It is ready to drink within months, if not days, of fermentation. Much of this produce has been stabilized to death by the time it is put on the market and is equally impervious to boiling or freezing. Otherwise of course it would be unequal to the tribulations of shipment and mass merchandising it must endure after it

clarity mania

leaves the winery. The American mania for perfect clarity in our beverages induces even our premium-wine producers to overtreat even their best wines. Most of the shiny equipment you will find in modern wineries is not used for making wine but for filtering and stabilizing it so that it will stay perfectly brilliant. Much of the fresh fruity grape aroma and flavor is inevitably sacrificed to avoid any sort of sediment which might offend the eye of the mighty American consumer.

How the desired degree of clarity and stabilization is achieved in our mass-produced *ordinaire* we shall leave to your imagination. The technology of mass-producing wine is very different anyway: Pasteurization, heat treatment to extract the red color from grapeskins before rather than during fermentation, and similar shortcuts are common practice. Let us, therefore, leave the mysterious methods of these manufacturers veiled in a decent obscurity. By way of reassurance, we hasten to add that their operations have absolutely nothing in common with those of which Addison (or was it Steele?) so quoteably complained over two hundred years ago:

technology today

"There is in this city a certain fraternity of chemical operators, who work underground in holes, caverns, and dark retirements, to conceal their mysteries from the eyes and observation of mankind. These subterraneous philosophers are daily employed in the transmutations of liquors, and by the power of magical drugs and incantations, raising under the streets of London the choicest products of the hills and valleys of France. They can squeeze Bordeaux out of the sloe, and draw Champagne from an apple. Virgil, in that remarkable prophecy,

. . . and of yore

'The ripening grape shall hang on every thorn'
seems to have hinted at this art, which can turn a plantation of northern hedges into a vineyard. These adepts are known among one another by the name of *Wine-brewers;* and, I am afraid, do great injury, not only to her Majesty's customs, but to the bodies of many of her good subjects." Modern industrial standardization notwithstanding, bottle for bottle American

ordinaire is easily the most palatable the world produces today, and none of it is chemical counterfeit.

A more inspiring subject by far is the making of Champagne and sparkling wines generally. The classical method, *la méthode champenoise,* took over a century to develop and is still being refined today. The vintner begins by blending a *cuvée* (tubful, literally) of his chosen white wines. All Champagne is a blend, and the quality of the wines blended is the all-important factor: Champagne can be no better than the wine that's used. Each vintner creates a blend of his own to constitute the *cuvée*. To the *cuvée* he adds a special Champagne yeast and about twenty pounds of sugar for each one hundred gallons of wine. The yeast goes to work on the sugar, and the wine begins to ferment for a second time. It is bottled immediately, and the bottles are sealed with crown caps or with corks that are fastened down with steel clamps. They are stacked horizontally in tiers and left undisturbed for many months. This time the carbonic gas generated by fermentation has no way to escape. The bottles become bombs, the pressure often equalling a hundred pounds to the square inch. Finally the gas becomes a component of the wine itself and the wine becomes effervescent. It is now Champagne.

"la méthode champenoise

This secondary fermentation can take anywhere from a few weeks to a few months. It produces the much-prized bubbles, but it also produces a deposit of solid particles, dead yeast cells mainly, which are trapped in the bottle. To filter the wine would remove the sparkle along with the debris. Dom Pérignon, who is credited with the invention of Champagne while he was cellar master at the Benedictine Abby of Hautvillers from 1668 to 1715, never solved this problem. For over a hundred years people simply tried to ignore the sediment in their champagne. Finally a lady both fastidious and ingenious devised a way to get rid of it. The lady was a widow named

its inventors

Clicquot, who carried on her husband's Champagne business after his death and who invented the last steps in *la méthode champenoise*.

After the secondary fermentation is completed, the wine is allowed to age on the yeast sediment. The longer it ages, the more of the characteristic Champagne flavor and bouquet it develops. Then it's ready for "riddling," or as the French call it, *remuage* ("moving"). The idea is to dislodge the sediment from the sides of the bottle and get it to collect on the cap or cork. The bottles are stood with their necks down in special racks. Every day each bottle is given a short, sharp spin and dropped back into place. The riddler or *remueur,* whose job this is, eventually becomes skillful enough to give perhaps fifty bottles a minute just the right turn. The operation is extremely delicate, and the fate of each bottle rests literally on a flick of his wrist. As the riddling goes on, the angle at which the bottles are standing is gradually increased. This process may go on for two weeks or three months depending on the batch of wine. When all the sediment finally rests against the cap or cork and the wine is brilliantly clear, the neck of the bottle is thrust into a brine solution which freezes the sediment and perhaps an inch of wine. The bottle is then opened and the pressure expels the frozen plug. The sediment, thanks to Madame Clicquot's inspiration, is gone! The Champagne is "disgorged."

At this point the wine is virtually without sugar and rather tart and astringent. A "Natural" Champagne is left this way, entirely undosed. Before recorking, all others receive a *dosage* which, like *remuage,* rhymes with garage. For obvious reasons most Champagne terminology is borrowed from the French. The *dosage*—a mixture of rock crystal sugar and brandy in wine—determines the Champagne's degree of sweetness or dryness and how it will be labelled. "Brut" will have up to .5 percent sugar, "Extra Dry" up to

"riddling"

what makes it pop

Champagne labelling

3 percent, and "Sec" up to 4. There's also "Demi-Sec" with 5 to 7 and "Doux" with up to 10 percent, but we hesitate to discuss such decoctions. Despite a loss of carbon dioxide during disgorging, the pressure remains somewhere between thirty and sixty pounds to the square inch inside the bottle, so the final cork is wired down with good reason. By the time it's ready to be chilled and served, French Champagne is usually at least five years old, somewhat more mature than American, though produced with no more care. Regardless of where it comes from, each bottle of Champagne produced by *la méthode champenoise* requires an estimated one hundred twenty hand operations, and at least one in every one hundred blows up before completing its curriculum.

blow up

In unusually good years the French Champagne producers "declare a vintage"—otherwise their wines bear no vintage dates. Those *cuvées spéciales* in which they have invested all their skill and prestige they also christen with special names. We generally look to Taittinger's vintaged *"Comtes de Champagnes,"* Moët & Chandon's *"Dom Pérignon,"* Piper-Heidsieck and Pol Roger for the best the French can do. Other leading French firms include Ayala, Bollinger, Charles Heidsieck, Heidsieck Monopole, Henriot, Krug, Lanson, Mumm, Perrier-Jouet, Pommery et Greno, Louis Roederer and Veuve Clicquot. There are perhaps thirty such firms altogether, and you won't find much to complain about a bottle from any of them. Unfortunately, the same cannot be claimed for American Champagne producers, who actually outnumber the French. "Champagne," of course, is not simply another way of saying "white sparkling wine," and the French government has only grudgingly acquiesced to our using the name, since virtually no other country does. But language is not subject to legislation: Americans do call white sparkling wines "Champagne," and the snobbish

the French situation

practice of putting quotation marks around the word when applied to any other than French wine is just an exercise in self-importance. But since the same name is used for wines of different origins, comparisons are inevitable.

Empire State Champagne

Nicholas Longworth of Cincinnati is the true father of New York Champagne. In 1845 he presented the world with 100,000 bottles of "Sparkling Catawba" made by the *méthode champenoise*. The most successful Eastern producers have continued to use both the time-honored techniques and the native-American *labrusca* grape varieties. The bubbly that results is as different from the taste of any other as a pear is from an apple, and just as good in its own right. The very driest New York Champagne is labelled *"brut* special," though some firms are content to label their driest simply *"brut."* "Special reserve" is midway between *"brut"* and "extra dry," which is actually the sweetest sold. The most highly regarded brand is probably Charles Fournier, followed by Gold Seal, Great Western, Taylor and Widmer.

Californian

California's finest dry Champagnes are some of her finest products and deserve to rank with their French cousins among the great wines of the world. They share a family resemblance, but the California wines are great not because of any similarities but because of their own merits: great dryness, strong scent and comparatively forceful, straightforward flavors. What the French are doing in California points up the distinction between the ideal French and the ideal Californian Champagne. Domaine Chandon, a subsidiary of the French-owned Moët & Chandon, has bought vineyards in the Carneros Creek area of the Napa Valley and will soon reach full production of 250,000 cases of bubbly per annum. Now in France, the Champagne cuvée uses only Chardonnay and Pinot Noir (yes, a black grape), with a touch of Pinot Meunier, which is ungrown here. The Old

World experts soon discovered, however, that Napa Chardonnay is quite distinct from the Chardonnay grown in their native Champagne. In the *its blend* cuvée for Domaine Chandon's quite good "Napa Valley Brut," they use Pinot Blanc liberally, thus taming the Chardonnay to "achieve a true Champagne-type character."

Well, hell, friends. Our life-long craving has turned up no Champagne "truer" than Californian; we find it as elegant as any "after," as Pound puts it, "another fashion that more suiteth me." But if French has the flavor you find *ne plus ultra,* our advice is to buy Schramsberg. You'll find it as French as the illegitimate daughters of Louis XIV. . . if you can find it at all. With *if you like the French,* perhaps a small assist from the President's having carried '69 Blanc de Blancs *you'll love . . .* to Peking and Moscow for toasting purposes, the exceptional qualities of Schramsberg creations make them our hardest-to-get-hold of. The maker of that Blanc de Blancs, Jack Davies, dubs it his "regular vintage"—80 percent Chardonnay, 20 percent Chenin Blanc, medium bodied and quite dry. He also now produces a fruity, brightly blushing Cuvée de Pinot and a demi-sec dessert Flora called Crémant. Mr. Davies' real virtuoso performance, in our opinion, is his Blanc de Noir, an elegant, pale-gold wine made almost entirely from the black Pinot Noir! Dry, full-bodied and complex puts it rather mildly. We also consider Llords & Elwood's fine Champagnes to be in a French style.

The French stop short of wholly "natural" Champagne, but in California at least six wineries have followed Korbel's lead in producing one. *but vive la différence* All because that Korbel Natural is so alive it's got a touch of wildness to it and tastes like the best brand of sunshine, subjectively speaking. And surely the world's best Champagne, Brut division, includes Sonoma Vineyards and the aforementioned Domaine Chandon—which has also produced a Blanc de

Noir in the Brut style—Weibel's Chardonnay Brut and Almadén's pink-salmon "Eye of the Partridge," each in its fresh particularity of difference. Mirassou has made a name for their unique Champagnes also, as has Hanns Kornell with his superb Extra Dry, among others.

California Champagne labels can be especially puzzling. The critical factors making for fine Champagne quality are two: use of the finest varieties of grapes, and extended aging of the wine on its yeast sediment after secondary fermentation. (French law requires vintaged Champagnes to be aged at least three years *en bouteille* before disgorging.) Now California labels will tell you nothing outright about either of these crucial elements. Your best guarantee of quality is the legend "fermented in this bottle"—not *the* but *this*. Hanns Kornell, Korbel, Mirassou, Oakville and others in this way distinguish their products from those of companies using a simplified version of the *méthode champenoise* called transfer process. This way Almadén and Paul Masson, among others, bypass the tedious riddling and disgorging stages in the Champagne process. A machine empties the bottles into a pressurized tank, sediment is then filtered out and the wine, with *dosage* added, is rebottled and corked. Since it undergoes bottle fermentation and aging, however, it is legally entitled to a "fermented in the bottle" label. The result isn't really bad, but *vive la différence* between the passable and best possible Champagne! It's exactly as one Champagne maker wrote to *Wines & Vines* magazine: " . . . the consumer is utterly in the dark and is being intentionally misled by producers using the transfer system."

Sparkling wines with the telltale words "bulk process" or "Charmat process" on their labels have little in common with any wines made by the *méthode champenoise*. They have no chance of being great and little chance of even being good. Most American Champagne, unfortunately, is

what isn't on the label

M. Charmat posthumously appraised

produced in this much faster and cheaper way. The wine has a rapid secondary fermentation in glass or stainless-steel tanks, relatively small ones as wine tanks go, that hold from fifty to one thousand gallons. The sediment is either left behind in the tank or removed by filter when the wine is bottled, under pressure, with the *dosage*. So much sediment develops that the taste of the wine is ruined by any prolonged contact with it, but without a chance for extended aging on yeast sediment, the wine cannot approximate any Champagne flavor. Christian Brothers and Masson are surprisingly good, but unpleasantly yeasty. Sour and raw are the kindest adjectives we can

what to do with it think of for the other bulk-process Champagnes we have tried. The one use for such stuff might be in that unbelievable drink of the nineteenth-century Irish gentry, Black Velvet. Black Velvet consists of equal amounts of Champagne and good Guinness stout and is obviously of Irish origin, being designed to buckle the knees and cross your eyes for you. Bulk-process Champagne does not harm the flavor of the stout at all. Mimosas are also possible.

No sparkling wine is cheap, because the Federal tax on them is twenty times greater than the tax on still table wines. Since you have to pay such excessive tariff for the bloody bubbles, doesn't it make sense to lay out

other sparkle plenties a little more for the wine around the bubbles? Excellent pink Champagnes are sometimes made by the *méthode champenoise,* but these, like sparkling Burgundy and Cold Duck, are for the most part bulk-process wines. Sparkling Burgundy is generally an inferior but pretty wine, popular with many non-wine drinkers who can't resist the combination of a certain sweetness and bubbles both in a red. Why anyone bought Cold Duck we cannot imagine, but they did. They don't anymore, much.

The most versatile and obliging of the fortified wines is Sherry, which takes its name from the Spanish town of Jerez de la Frontera, about one hundred twenty miles north of Gibraltar. The ancient name of the town was Xeres, and the Moors called it "Scherish." The region around Jerez produces not one or two or three, but dozens of different Sherries which may bear little or no resemblance to each other. The four most familiar imported types are: (1) *Fino.* Very dry, pale wine that may be served chilled as an aperitif or with food. Our favorites: Gonzales, Byass "Tio Pepe"; Pedro Domecq "La Ina"; Harvey's "Pale Dry Cocktail"; Duff Gordon's "Santa Maria." (2) *Amontillado.* Deeper in color, older, and somewhat more full-bodied than a *fino,* with a fragrance and lingering undertaste like toasted nuts. Our favorites: Duff Gordon "Amontillado"; Harvey's "Amontillado Pale Dry"; Sandeman's "Amontillado Fino." (3) *Dry Oloroso.* Very fragrant; full-bodied, and mellow. Our favorites: "Dry Sack"; Harvey's "Shooting Sherry"; Findlater, Mackie, Todd and Company's "Dry Fly." (4) *Dessert Oloroso.* Generally a dark golden amber, the richest and heaviest of Sherries. Our favorites: Harvey's "Bristol Cream"; Pedro Domecq's "Celebration Cream"; Duff Gordon's "Cream Sherry." There are numerous other Sherry shippers whose products, our friends assure us, are as good as any we have listed but these are the only ones for which we can speak from first-hand experience.

favorites

There is at least three times as much California Sherry as there is Spanish, but the only ones which more or less approximate the original generally carry the words *flor* and/or *solera* on their labels. These refer not to kinds of Sherry but to the way it is made. Once the wine is fermented to dryness, wine spirits are added to bring the alcohol content up to about 15 percent and then the *flor* yeast is introduced into the mixture. *Flor* is Spanish for "flower," for it flowers into a thick scum atop the wine as it ages in open vats or casks. (For some reason, Spanish *olorosos* grow little or no

flor

flor, however.) Only in the last decade or so have California wineries begun using *flor* yeast in their Sherry making. After the wine is fully impregnated with the *flor* flavors, it is brought up to full alcoholic strength, somewhere between 18 and 21 percent, and then drawn off into casks.

If the Sherry is made after the Spanish fashion, the casks are arranged into a *solera* system. A *solera* is basically a series of communicating barrels lying in superimposed rows four or five tiers high. The wine is not protected from the air but rather exposed to it, and to the contrasting heat of day and cool of night. Newer wine is always added to casks in the topmost tier of the *solera.* When the Sherry is judged fully mature and ready for bottling, just one-third to one-half a cask at a time is drawn off a bottom-tier cask. The bottom tier is replenished from the second row, and these in turn from the third, and so on. In its slow progress through the *solera* system, the new wine not only "marries" the old but also assumes its character. A remarkably small amount of old Sherry will "key" an enormous amount of young. This system of aging and blending enables a Sherry maker to market the same wine year after year because it all comes out of the same barrels. By the time it is withdrawn from a *solera,* the Sherry is a wonderfully harmonious and well-aged blend. Wineries that go to this much trouble to produce good Sherry usually use the Palomino grape from which Spanish Sherries are also made. The best California Sherries we've discovered come from Almadén, Brookside Vineyard, Llords & Elwood and Weibel. To this list we can now add Cresta Blanca's "Dry Watch," Buena Vista's "Ultra Dry" and Sebastiani's "Arenas Dry."

Names like *fino* or *oloroso* are not applied to California Sherry. "Cream" Sherry represents a California attempt at a dessert *oloroso,* the richest, sweetest sort. "Golden" usually denotes a slightly drier, lighter-

solera

best California Sherries

111

bodied wine. In descending order of dryness we then have "Sherry," "dry Sherry," "cocktail Sherry," and "pale dry Sherry." But every winery is *Sherry names* allowed to juggle these names at will or to invent new ones, so occasionally a "cocktail Sherry" may be paler and drier than a "pale dry." If the label doesn't specify *flor* or *solera,* you must be guided by the winery's reputation. Beaulieu, Martini and Sebastiani, to name a few we've tried, all produce (by whatever method) a fairly creditable Sherry.

If the winery has no reputation, you may assume you're merely buying a cheap, strong wine. Most of it is made by the so-called "baking" method. The basic wine is fermented to the desired degree of dryness, then spirits are added to check fermentation and preserve the remaining sugar content. The wine is then kept for a number of months at around 120 degrees Fahrenheit in the hope that the resulting oxidation will make it taste like Sherry. It doesn't—though the best of these do rather resemble Madeira.

It is this fortification with alcohol to arrest fermentation of the grape *fortification* sugar which is responsible for the greater alcoholic strength of aperitif and dessert wines generally. We have neither space not time, as the man who was put in a sack and drowned said, to account for the existence of Angelica, Madeira, Malaga, Marsala, Tokay and white Port. We've never encountered an American-made wine by these names we could recommend to anybody.

Ports in California California Ports and Muscatels can be more rewarding. The best Ports seem to be produced from the Tinta Madeira grape. The Portuguese product generally makes California's version taste very bland, indelicate, and overly sweet in comparison. Ficklin, Paul Masson and the Novitiate of Los Gatos— and more recently J.W. Morris, Quady and Woodbury—produce excellent Port, and prove by example that good California Port is at least possible. "Ruby" Port is younger and far redder than "tawny" Port, which has to be

aged in the wood long enough to turn russet or almost brown. Muscat and *Muscats*
Muscatel wines are among the sweetest and most ancient of all. They have a
perfume and flavor unmistakably their own. Portugal, or more exactly the
city of Setúbal in Portugal, is the leading producer of fine Muscat wines. The
variety known as Muscat de Frontignan in France or Moscato di Canelli in
Italy is the one that produces the most distinctive California Muscat wines.
Concannon, Charles Krug, Papagni, Robert Mondavi and San Martin
seem to do best by this distinctive family of grapes. "Muscatel" is only the
most familiar of the several kinds of Muscat wine made. There is also
light-sweet Muscat, dry Muscat, cream of Muscat and sparkling Muscat.

No treatise on wine making can omit all mention of brandy. No *brandy recipe*
doubt the most useful thing to know about it is how to make good old
brandy out of positively vile stuff.

(1) Pour it through the air into a large receptacle—from the top of
the stairs into a bathtub below, for instance.

(2) Put it into bottles, with a plum in each bottle.

(3) Stand it up with no corks in the bottles for some two or three
days, even a week—or two or three weeks.

(4) Put a drop of maraschino into each bottle.

The bottles are now old brandy, and you can give them funny names
and drink it out of big glasses and roll it around, warming it with your hands
and smelling at it like a dog.

This advice of Hilaire Belloc's need not be followed in the case of
two California brandies at least—Christian Brothers XO Reserve and
Setrakian. Truly superb, they are the only Californian brandy wines that can
satisfy even confirmed old Armagnac-addicted palates like ours.

WINE HISTORY
What's new?

(A history of wine)   . . . would need infinite research to satisfy my own ideas of thoroughness: for I have never yet given a second-hand opinion of anything or book or person. Also, I should have had to drink more good wine than would now be good for my pocket or perhaps even my health, and more bad than I could contemplate without dismay in my advancing years.

—George Saintsbury

entral heating and running water are not the only comforts the world forgot about when the Roman Empire collapsed beneath the onslaught of barbarian tribes. Lost also was that great comfort to the spirit, mature wine. There is no shortage of classical poets who testify in praise of wine, wine of every sort. One of the most difficult and endearing of them is Horace, the son of a slave who became the intimate of Augustus, the ruler of the world. His poems are devoid of snobbism; he's able to extol the Emperor's finest vintages and still invite him over for a bottle of *ordinaire* offered without apology.

Wine was plentiful in the ancient world and formed part of a slave's daily ration. The price for *ordinaire* in Rome over the years averaged about a dime per gallon. The better sorts of wine were put up in amphorae, which were then sealed, labelled and stored to age. Greek vintages reached maturity in about seven years; many of the Italian wines required twenty. As an aid to preservation the ancients often added turpentine or something similar—the Romans coated the insides of the amphora with pine pitch—to produce something on the order of retsina, which is the national wine of Greece to this day. But this was not the practice with all wines. The amphora, a porous pottery vessel stoppered with plaster or wax, allowed the wine to breathe and thus to go on getting better until it was as good as it could be.

When unresinated wine was inadequately preserved in the amphora—no unusual thing in ancient Italy—it turned to vinegar, and when vinegar exposed to the air lost its acidity, it became completely insipid. Such slop *"wop"* was called in Latin *vappa* (pronounced woppa) and the Romans used the word figuratively for any no-account person. This name for a good-for-nothing still persists in Neapolitan dialect and appears as "woppo." Applied years ago as a term of abuse by one New York Italian about another, it entered American slang as "wop," the standard racial slur flung at Italians. Besides red and white the ancients had brown wine, which the world has done without very nicely ever since.

Rich Romans of the first century A.D. had as large and varied a repertoire of wines to draw on as the wealthy have today, and the *nouveau riche* among them displayed the famous names and "right" years whenever they could obtain them. Trimalchio, for example, in that most fantastic of ancient stories, Petronius's *Satyricon,* claims to serve his guests the most notoriously expensive wine of the period. "'Falernian from the year of Opimius's consulship, a hundred years in the bottle!' And as we were reading the labels, Trimalchio clapped his hands and cried, 'Alas that wine should live longer than we wretched men! Let's wet our whistles–wine is life.'" The pretentious old Trimalchio was probably lying; Opimian vintage (121 B.C.) would actually have been much older. Pliny the Elder, who outlived Petronius thirteen years to perish with Pompeii, says: "There was such a blaze of hot weather that in that year the grapes were literally cooked–cooking is the technical word--by the sun and the wines made last to this day after nearly two hundred years."

ancient connoisseurship

Two hundred and fifty years after the last Emperor stepped down from his throne, his realms had been divided between the Christian Pope in the West and the Islamic Caliph in the East. Their opposing views were almost equally barren: the Moslem practice favored plenty of women but absolutely no wine, whereas the Catholic ideal permitted plenty of wine but no women. The Dark Ages are rightly so-called. Life might have proved altogether impossible in Europe but for the late Roman invention of the

barbarism
and the barrel

117

barrel. Wooden barrel staves must be exactly coopered so as to fit together and bent so that pressure is exerted equally throughout. Then the heads must be fitted such that the whole is proof against leakage—no mean engineering achievement. People would sometimes put wine in jugs stopped up with straw and with a layer of olive oil on top of it to protect it from the air, but mainly they kept their wine in barrels. The wine had to be drunk quickly, before it had a chance to turn to vinegar, which it often did even before the next year's vintage was in. There was a perennial shortage of wine, and the scholarly medieval poets, with a combination of thirst and piety, constantly besought their patrons for supplies when they ran out of wine and bitter beer raged in their bellies.

As the feudal period drew to its unlamented end, the trade in wine picked up. Quality was never high, perhaps, by modern (or ancient) standards, but people learned to distinguish different regional wines and merchants learned to fool their customers. Climatic changes had rendered England unfit for grape growing, though the Romans had pursued viticulture successfully there. Forced to import their wines, the English became more sophisticated wine drinkers than their contemporaries who were able to satisfy themselves with home production. Chaucer has his Pardoner, a confessed beer drinker, begin his tale

Chaucer's advice

> Now keep ye from the white and from the red,
> And namely from the white wine of Lepe,
> That is to sell in Fish Street or in Chepe.
> This wine of Spain creepeth subtilly
> In other wines, growing fast by,
> Of which there riseth such fumositee,
> That when a man has drunken draughtes three
> And weneth that he be at home in Chepe,
> He is in Spain, right at the town of Lepe,
> Not at the Rochelle nor at Bordeaux town.

Lepe, the modern Niebla located not far from Seville, evidently produced a strong cheap wine which was sold under its own name in Chaucer's London and which was also used for adulterating better wines from Bordeaux and La Rochelle. Its "fumositee"–delightful word!–found its way into the weaker French wines and got you drunk the quicker. The fumes of the wine then transported the inebriate not to Bordeaux or La Rochelle where they supposedly came from but to Lepe, the home of the strong wine predominant in the mixture. The Middle Ages and Renaissance added all manner of honey and herbs to their wines to mask their defects and render them potable, and the sweeter the wine, the more it was valued in those cold and sugarless days. A young Beaujolais or rosé will give some idea of the very best unadulterated wine most men of those times could hope to come by, and that not too often.

The chief source of England's beverage continued for three hundred years to be Bordeaux. The generally mediocre quality of this short-lived and light-colored wine is obvious from its name *Clairette,* which the English with their sovereign disdain for other people's spelling called Claret. All this was changed about the beginning of the eighteenth century when England, being on the outs with the aged Louis Quatorze, concluded a treaty with the Portuguese whereby their wines could enter Britain paying a much lower import duty than the French. The only difficulty English policy and the Portuguese merchants encountered came from the wine itself. So horribly harsh and dry was it, no Englishman wanted to buy it at any price. The

Port and fortification

merchants at Oporto learned to fortify their product with brandy and thus to check fermentation and retain in the wine sufficient sugar to make it palatable. This expedient was discovered and first put into practice sometime between 1725 and 1730, but more was needed. The wine and alcohol required time to amalgamate and throw off impurities. The solution was a second stroke of genius: bottling the wine and corking the bottles.

drinking stars

But to give honor where it's due, we must backtrack a bit and mention Dom Pérignon, supposedly the very first to hit upon the cork-and-bottle idea. "Come quickly," the blind monk is supposed to have cried, "I'm drinking stars." He had invented Champagne. Grapes ripen slowly in the Champagne district and must be harvested late. Having a fairly low sugar content, they also ferment slowly. The winter cold arrests the fermentation process until springtime warms the wine, and it begins to ferment again. Dom Pérignon blended the wines from his neighborhood and then bottled the blend as it began to undergo its secondary fermentation. The gas given off by fermentation had to remain dissolved in the wine, awaiting release in the form of bubbles once the bottle was uncorked. Most of the good monk's bottles exploded, of course, and another century had to pass before somebody found a way to get the sediment out of the Champagne. Sparkling wine, therefore, only became fashionable and widely known long after Port. When Dom Pérignon departed this vale of tears in 1715, he left it immeasureably happier and richer, not only for Champagne but also for the cork, which the purveyors of Port were so soon to popularize.

a century passes

This is a fitting point in our story to give thanks for this "most important event in the history of fine wine," the invention of the cork. Wine, as we have seen, requires air to stay alive. But there comes a point when wine left in the wood begins to oxidize too fast, to "burn up." In its cask it would become emaciated and tired long before reaching maturity. Put in a bottle and allowed no more air than seeps through a cork, good wine goes on improving slowly until it achieves the fulfillment of all its innate potential. When next you get the chance to enjoy a fine wine, properly aged, reflect that this is a pleasure mankind did without for fifteen hundred years until we came up with an equivalent to the classical stoppered amphora.

the invention of the cork

The cork revolutionized the drinking and appreciation of wine in the course of the eighteenth century. Watteau's paintings show that wine in the bottle was known at the French Court by the time of his death in 1727. And a few among the British aristocracy began to appreciate the fine points in the wines becoming available to them, as the copious correspondence of those pre-telephone days will testify. One Lord Carlisle writes George Augustus

Selwyn, one of society's trend setters at the time: "I wish you would speak to Foxcroft in case he should have a pipe of exceeding good Claret, to save it for me. I do not mean that you shall have anything to do with choosing it for me, for you can drink ink and water if you are told it is Claret. Get somebody who understands it to taste it for you." Only the wealthy could afford to cultivate a taste for Claret or the other French wines in that period.

18th century tastes The reasonably priced beverage wines were not French. Rhine wines gained great popularity, and since much of it was shipped from Hochheimer, national habit compelled the English to call all Rhine wine "Hock." But the eighteenth century was not a time of delicacy and refinement, and though they were fond of wine, often disastrously so, most people were far more concerned with quantity than with quality, and took more interest in the kick the wine promised than its more subtle and artistic aspects. The spirit of the time is apparent in a song from Sheridan's *School for Scandal* which we like well enough to quote.

> Here's to the maiden of bashful fifteen,
> Now to the widow of fifty;
> Here's to the flaunting extravagant queen,
> And here's to the housewife that's thrifty.
> Let the toast pass—drink to the lass!
> I warrant she'll prove an excuse for the glass.

The song goes on proposing toasts for four more stanzas, with always the same refrain.

The Age of Port For the English it was pre-eminently the Age of Port. Horace Walpole, the foremost letter writer of his day, refers nowhere in his correspondence to a château or vintage year but mentions Port constantly. He writes, for instance, that doctors were much impressed by the case of Charles

Mildmay, Lord Fitzwalter, who was still alive in December, 1755. He was past eighty-four, had been a great ladies' man and, according to Horace, "had scarce ever more sense than he has at present." For many months he had been thriving on fourteen barrels of oysters, seven bottles of brandy, and two-dozen bottles of Port a week.

Lo! The nineteenth century—the Golden Age of Wine the English call it. In the ninety-nine years between the day Napoleon retired in defeat from the field of Waterloo and that on which German forces struck across Belgium at France, Europe knew no general war. Uprisings aplenty, but these were local matters. The Crimean and Franco-Prussian conflicts were self-contained and neatly concluded bloodbaths that did little more than give the bourgeoisie at home something diverting to discuss. And with the growth of industrialism they were meantime making more and more money and spending more and more of it on wines. Even the not-so-wealthy had space and time to lay down bottles for twenty or thirty years. The Russian troops opposing Napoleon in the Waterloo campaign had been quartered in Champagne. They plundered all the cellars of the district and carried an unquenchable thirst for Champagne back home with them to the steppes. The fashion gradually spread to other countries too, but the Champagne merchants recovered far more than their losses from the Russian market alone over the century that ensued.

Champagne

Claret was once again the standard wine of Englishmen. Everyone with any pretention to social standing affected connoisseurship. The Bordeaux *châteaux* became name brands, and it was mainly to publicize the Bordeaux wines—and to enhance their snob appeal—that their wily French promoters devised the notorious "Classification of 1855." The Bordeaux Chamber of Commerce commissioned a group of brokers to draw up a list of

Classification of 1855

the best vineyards to represent the region at the Universal Exhibition in Paris. They came up with sixty-five *châteaux*—as even the most modest of Bordeaux wineries may be called—which they ranked in five categories or "growths." This classification has probably done more to swell the ranks of the wine snobs than anything before or since. The classification was based on price and intended to single out the wines which had, on the average, commanded the highest prices up to that time. From then 'til now the Bordeaux merchants and exporters have been able to exploit the reputation of these these "growths" or *crus,* and thus they have remained the most expensive. Although the experts responsible for the classification emphasized that it was provisional and would go out of date, their list was only altered for the first time in 1973 when Château Mouton-Rothschild was elevated to the ranks of *premier grand cru.*

les crus

By the middle of the century, more wine was being produced—and more being aged—than ever before in Europe. According to educated estimates, at least 25 percent of it spoiled before completing fermentation, but much of what survived must have been extraordinary. The Victorians seldom spoke in superlatives except when it came to the wines they loved. The wine trade was thus at its zenith in Europe by the time another chapter in wine history was well underway in the New World.

something else indeed

We have elsewhere given an account of wine pioneering in this country down to recent times, when the American people as a whole began rushing to the wine shop as if to an assignation. Future historians of the subject may diligently inquire why this happened in our times instead of two hundred or even twenty-five years ago and a large part of their answer will surely be found in technology. This technology and the wine rush combined

have permitted wine men to pursue their ideal wines. This is what makes our present era in wine history a truly revolutionary one.

wine idealists

Bob and Elinor Travers' Mayacamas winery (and home) is located in the crater of an extinct volcano and they make astonishing wines there. Over a bottle of their '72 Late Harvest Zinfandel—"the second miracle of Mayacamas," to quote R. L. Balzer—we were speculating as to the wine's life expectancy when Mr. Travers said: "There's just no way to know. Only two others like it have ever been made."

To generalize about such new developments, start with the actual owners of today's wineries. We wrote in 1971: ". . . the alarmists are no longer alone in fearing the eclipse, if not the demise, of the family-owned winemaking operation with generations-old traditions of excellence." Already at that time, National Distillers owned Almadén, Seagram owned Paul Masson, Beaulieu Vineyard and Inglenook had recently been acquired by Heublein. The list of corporate and conglomerate-acquired wineries has since

corporate owners

grown to include Beringer, Buena Vista, Brookside, Cambiaso, Cucamonga, Cuvaison, Franzia, San Martin, Simi and Sterling, and now there are nearly thirty in all. The worry was whether corporations could accept the fact that wine is a personal, indeed a tempermental, product to produce. Apparently they've had to. Heublein, for instance, mucked about with Inglenook wines for several years. Wine journalists and gossips discovered with dismay a decline in the quality of their varietal reds, especially, until several years hence management once again decided that only fanatics should be allowed to make wine after all, if you want people to wax fanatical about them. This is a good thing, for fine wine can never be mass-produced. Fine wine, like any artistic creation, is the result of individual skill and applied talent. Making great wine is something else again. Bob Travers put it most elegantly on the afternoon already mentioned: "The freer from defects you want your wines, the safer you play it. For great wine you run risks, take chances. It takes a combination of guts and lunacy." As it turns out, our fears for the dedicated risk-runner prove groundless. Besides which, privately owned and fanatic-run wineries have proliferated more rapidly than ever these last few years. Over a hundred new ones have appeared since 1975.

risk-running

Fortunately different wine men are fanatical on different points and taken together, therefore, account for a wide range of new trends affecting the quality of what we drink. The Sebastiani winery ranks as California's eighth largest (just ahead of Christian Brothers) and is committed to a one-winery campaign to prevent the criminal consumption of fine red wines years before they're ready for drinking. They only release those approaching their peak of drinkability and this aging program has produced any number of wines we could dwell on lovingly. Beaulieu seems also to have decided upon aging the better part of their finest before sale. Tax laws that don't penalize aging wines on a winery's premises just went into effect in 1970, and the glut of wine to come can only induce others to take advantage of them. The number of *magnificos* ready to drink is bound to multiply.

the well aged

Parducci, on the other hand, would have very few reds to sell if theirs were held for fullest maturity. Their 1968—and first—bottling of Cabernet Sauvignon has only just emerged from its adolescence. It marked the first time anybody in California had ever produced an unfined and unfiltered version of this variety. As champions of minimal-to-no monkeying with wine, we are reminded with boring regularity that wine may be filtered and remain fine nonetheless. That's true. But a lot more could be fine and much finer if it were not subjected to the rigors of aroma-removing, character-destroying filtration which strips the precious stuff of much flavor, body and

the unfiltered truth

aging potential we hold dear. Chappellet, Carneros Creek, Mirassou, Robert Mondavi, Sterling and ZD—a most exclusive list!—are among those who have to date concurred and produced unfined and/or unfiltered reds. So what if it's 1990 when some of these attain full perfection: they're demonstrably worth waiting for already and we will need great wines more than ever then.

The ancient art of blending is also due for a revival. Generics are always blends, of course, and for years you could count on five fingers such California Chablis and Burgundy as rose to any distinction whatever. Varietal labelling clearly indicated the direction of quality twenty years ago and the public has finally been educated to look for varietal names—another good thing. Nowadays we must also realize there's no virtue in slavishly sticking on one-variety winemaking for its own sake. Who wouldn't prefer a splendid *innovative* blended wine to a second-rate Pinot Noir, say, an easy example because most *blending* Pinot Noirs suffer blahs when left on their own. Why not blend it with a number of other varieties in such cases and create a whole new wine? As long as it's outstanding it hardly matters what you call it. That's the way the Mirassous see it, too. "White Burgundy" is the new name they've given their less-than-satisfactory Pinot Blanc, along with a new oaky style and an infusion of Chenin Blanc and French Colombard.

Other wineries have also demonstrated conclusively that generic wines need not taste like sheep in sheep's clothing. In 1967 Buena Vista's Al Brett put together a wine named Lachrymae Montis after the "Claret" General Vallejo made on the property for his personal consumption (and served Haraszthy to illustrate Sonoma's wine-growing potential). Sebastiani's *inspired examples* '67 Burgundy was an inspired blend of Carignane, Petite Sirah and Zinfandel which time married perfectly . . . superb stuff, so good you really wondered if any other wine man in the state had anything near August Sebastiani's genius for blending. Beaulieu's 1968 Burgundy Special was of comparable stature, however, and since then Christian Brothers' master blender Bud Berg delivered his first "Brother Timothy Special Selections." Each Christian Brothers varietal has been a blend, invariably nicely harmonized. From their huge inventory of wines, they combined different Zinfandels, say, in different proportions to come up with a wine that's much superior to the sum of its parts. Those ideally aged Special Selections were completely convincing testimony in favor of more such blending.

The law permits a varietally labelled wine to contain up to 49 percent of other varieties—25 percent if vintage-dated—but in some cases this laxity may become the key to finer varietals. Californians have heard Cabernet Sauvignon called "the noble grape of Bordeaux" so long we're in danger of believing it's the only one they've got. Yet the vineyards of Château Lafite-Rothschild are only about five-eighths Cabernet Sauvignon; the remainder is planted to Cabernet Franc and Merlot. Much St. Emilion and Pomerol, moreover, is made exclusively from Merlot. We've long since accepted the world's judgement that at its best our Cabernet Sauvignon ranks with the world's greatest red wines. The question is how our vintners can bring more of it to that "at best" standard and raise some even higher. The answer, we submit, will in many cases be Merlot.

Cabernet at best

Freemark Abbey's 1968 was the first Californian Cabernet to be blended with Merlot we're told; the amount used was minuscule—3.14 percent—and the wine aged in small Nevers oak cooperage. The result, in trusty old Leon Adams' words, was "the first California red wine I have thus far tasted that might be mistaken for a good vintage of Château Margaux." Freemark Abbey's practice of blending Merlot with their Cabernet dates from this experiment. The best we've tried was a 1974 named Cabernet

Merlot

Bosché after John Bosché, whose 15-acre vineyard is the exclusive source of the grapes. It was beyond suspicion of imperfection—fairly big, ripe-flavored wine with all the complexity of a late Beethoven fugue and already smooth enough to enjoy though it had been neither fined nor filtered! That's the difference 10 percent Merlot can make. It imparts a morbifuge complexity and softness and renders the wine drinkable much earlier. Donn Chappellet and the good people at Beaulieu, Sterling, Veedercrest and elsewhere have begun blending it into their Cabernet to take advantage of these qualities. Each of their bottlings released to date has been memorably successful and the trend they've started is bound to continue. The 3,600 acres of Merlot standing in 1980 represents almost forty times the acreage available in 1970.

Making sense of contemporary wine history requires a great deal of raw data like the foregoing and too much of it, you will have noticed, rapidly becomes rather a bore. In a similar predicament James Agee wrote something worth our quoting here: "If I bore you, that is that. If I am clumsy, that may indicate partly the difficulty of my subject and the seriousness with which I am trying to take what hold I can of it."

How do you take hold of a pronouncement like Robert Mondavi's recent one, "The Golden Age of California wine lies just ahead"? His words have all the *veritas* there is *in vino,* but we must uncork many a bottle by way of proving the point. These bottles will oftentimes illustrate the technical expertise winemakers are now for the first time able to take for granted, just as in pre-Pasteur days they took it as a matter of course that much wine would spoil during and after fermentation. Pause before pouring your next bottle of Mirassou Chenin Blanc or Johannisberg Riesling and reflect that the first time that wine or the must from which it's made was exposed to the air was the instant you uncorked the bottle. Within seconds

what did he say?

131

of being picked these grapes were stemmed and crushed and the juice stored in tanks blanketed with carbon dioxide gas (whose only effect is to protect it from air contact), all by one and the same machine. Labor-saving apart, its chief contribution is that it captures the full fragrance of the grape. Upright Harvesters have found many more customers for their machine since the Mirassous first demonstrated its value.

new technologies

Recently developed "cold fermentation" procedures permit incredibly delicate handling of white wines—Parducci's French Colombard and Bob Mondavi's famous Fumé Blancs are only a few examples of wines that could not have been created without it. Unfiltered wines are not new and neither, as we have seen, are ideally aged or blended ones. Never before this decade have California wines like them appeared on the general market, however, and the harbingers we've cited are worthy of any Golden Age. Technological breakthroughs like the ones we've mentioned are heralds also, but most decisive of all for history-making purposes is the individual winemaker's combination of guts and lunacy. For sheer fanaticism in pursuit of quality, their equals, man for man, would be hard to find anywhere in the country today.

Your 24-karat Golden Ages of Wine eventually require a definable and reliable selection of unsurpassable wines such as the Romans had and such as Bordeaux's Classification of 1855 was meant to provide. This became the foundation for the present system of *appellation contrôlée* in France, which is basically a codification of what's been known since Roman days there: Pinot Noirs grow better in Burgundy generally and best of all in specific parcels of Burgundian *terroir,* for example. By now this system has been honed to such extraordinary precision we can claim the world's best Burgundy comes from a specific four and one-half acres of ground whereon the Pinot Noir seldom yields even four tons to the acre. At, say, 120 gallons of finished wine to the ton, the very most the Romanée-Conti vineyard can produce in a year is 900 cases. For most of us it might as well be legendary.

Today's California wines with the stuff of legend in them are just beginning to be identified, as with Bosché's Cabernet, and the quality fanatics are developing a semisystem of appellation of their own. Some have tried a scientific approach and others, with equal success, play their hunches. Wine columnist Lindy Linquist observed: "While it was science that correctly said the Salinas Valley (in Monterey County) would be great grape-growing ground, it was also science that told Bernard Fetzer when he built his winery in the hills of Mendocino County that no vine would survive the first winter." We have Fetzer's hunch to thank for the fine wines he's produced there. They share their Redwood Valley appellation of origin with wines made by the single man most responsible for this appellation movement, John Parducci. What he's unleashed upon us is going to produce important changes in wine labels in the not-too-distant future. Most "North Coast" or even "Napa Valley" Pinot Noirs may be disappointments, but one labelled "Carneros" will always mean a good bet. That's just one of the individual wine addresses the government is being asked to approve for Napa County. There's also Spring Mountain, Mt. Veeder, Oakville, St. Helena, and Yountville so far . . . already provocation enough for generation-long debates! Simi has already gotten "Alexander Valley" designated in Sonoma, where at least six more localities and microclimates have been proposed. Vineyardists as far south as San Diego have begun clamoring for protection of their local names.

California's appellation movement

tomorrow's classics

At this moment the appellation movement is bureaucracy-bound and hog-tied well past hope, it would appear. The IRS's Bureau of Alcohol,

Tobacco and Firearms only responds with yea or nay after some vintner has made a claim. It's not a very happy anarchy because, for one thing, the BATF doesn't really know how to evaluate and legally define the assortment of valleys and vineyards proposed. The federales want the states to assume this function since local authorities should be the ones most intimately familiar with local geography. Then what's to keep Ohio from recognizing a legal Napa Valley there? is the reply. This hassle has a life expectancy better than thine or ours. That an appellation system will develop nonetheless, not even the most casual consumer of California grapeblood can doubt. It will all seem very neat and tidy by then, and your liquor store will supply complimentary Monterey County vintage charts.

the proof-bringing

For the California wine drinker, in short, these are already exciting times and talk of their getting more "Golden" may sound like rankest boosterism to anyone else. Having touched on the most recent and important trends toward higher quality, we've said enough anyway. "We have no will to try proof-bringing," as Ezra Pound claimed about love. For that there are great wines aplenty for those who know how to recognize them. Our best assurance of the future of quality in wine rests with the earth itself, which ennobles those who work it: The soil is on the side of nobility. Truly fine wines will always be scarce, but old Bacchus and his colleague St. Vincent, the patron saint of wine and winemaking, will see to it there's a supply.

WINE VARIETIES
What are we drinking anyhow?

There are Thasian vines, there are white Mareotic;
The first thrive on fat terroir, the second on poorer soil.
Also there's the Psithian, useful in raisin wines, and
Light Lagean, someday sure to trip and tongue-tie you.
And Purple and Precian and you, Rhaetian, how
Am I to bottle your poetry?
Compare yourself not with finest Falernian though!
From Aminnean vines come the soundest of wines
Which Tmolian and even the kingly Chian bow before;
There's the minor Argitis which surpasses all others
Alike in yield of juice and length of life.
Nor shall I pass you by, vine of Rhodes,
Prized by banqueting men and gods with the second course
Nor, Bumastis, you with your swelling clusters.
There is no number for the many kinds
And names of wines there are . . . .

—Virgil

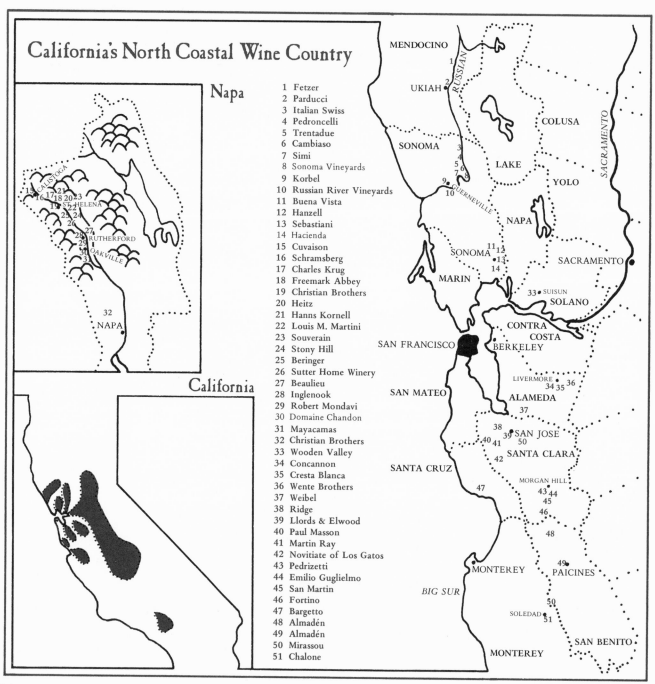

California's North Coastal Wine Country

Napa

California

1 Fetzer
2 Parducci
3 Italian Swiss
4 Pedroncelli
5 Trentadue
6 Cambiaso
7 Simi
8 Sonoma Vineyards
9 Korbel
10 Russian River Vineyards
11 Buena Vista
12 Hanzell
13 Sebastiani
14 Hacienda
15 Cuvaison
16 Schramsberg
17 Charles Krug
18 Freemark Abbey
19 Christian Brothers
20 Heitz
21 Hanns Kornell
22 Louis M. Martini
23 Souverain
24 Stony Hill
25 Beringer
26 Sutter Home Winery
27 Beaulieu
28 Inglenook
29 Robert Mondavi
30 Domaine Chandon
31 Mayacamas
32 Christian Brothers
33 Wooden Valley
34 Concannon
35 Cresta Blanca
36 Wente Brothers
37 Weibel
38 Ridge
39 Llords & Elwood
40 Paul Masson
41 Martin Ray
42 Novitiate of Los Gatos
43 Pedrizetti
44 Emilio Guglielmo
45 San Martin
46 Fortino
47 Bargetto
48 Almadén
49 Almadén
50 Mirassou
51 Chalone

his chapter will be unfair, unabashedly prejudiced, and worth reading twice. The only thing riskier than trusting a guide to wines is buying them without any guidance at all. Most especially is this true when it comes to special wines, as now we have. Every one of the multifarious ways of comparing, ranking and recommending wine has something wrong with it. For ours we claim only that it's meant to be useful and based on the principle that a sample is better than a sermon. Look elsewhere for laborious scorings and wordy tasting notes. This is not meant to be an historical document recording judgements of certain vintages and varietals from certain wineries. Such a book goes out of date before it gets into print. Not only have many of the wines considered disappeared from the merchants' shelves, but the ones remaining will have gotten better or worse in the interim, for wines and human beings never stay the same.

One is always reduced to generalizations in writing about wine and there is always an element of risk in choosing one. Every wine bibber has discoveries, surprises and disappointments to tell about, and this is the record of ours brought up to date. Our notes on the several thousand California wines we've consumed since the first edition of this book appeared are chiefly valuable for the patterns they reveal. No amount of past experience can tell us (or you) exactly how Beaulieu's next vintage of Pinot Noir will turn out relative to Pedroncelli's. But experience has shown us that they will usually rank with the best and are therefore always worth checking out. We single out such wines as favorites and our choices represent intensely personal appreciations. Our prejudices are obvious enough, but take note, too, of our unfairness in omitting many a candidate from consideration.

With only fourteen meals in the week and a limit to how much one can drink with any meal, however, we assure you that we have done our utmost. Consider the sacrifice of sobriety required. A financial factor has also influenced our choice of favorites: What may be a splendid wine indeed for $3.50 calls for a lot more thought if it costs $7. You may be sure any favorites we mention costing more than that have to be damned extraordinary. We feel Californian Sherry, Champagne and Port can be evaluated only in comparison with their European prototypes and in terms of the way they're made; our preferred brands have therefore been listed in the chapter on winemaking.

CHARDONNAY
[Shar'-doe-nay]

The Chardonnay is a glorious grape. It is cultivated most extensively in Burgundy and the tiny Chablis area in France, where it produces white wines you would sell your soul for. In Champagne to the north it is grown along with Pinot Noir for use in Champagne, and around Mâcon to the South it produces that fine wine, Pouilly-Fuissé. It may have been raised by the Romans in all of these districts. The aristocratic Chardonnay is one of the three or four grapes capable of producing truly great white wines in California. Though a full-bodied wine with a pungent perfume, it has the delicacy of crystal and is smooth as frog's fur in the mouth. People speak of it as having an "apple-like" aroma, but we have found this not always the case. You can, however, almost invariably detect the flavors of the oak in which it was aged. The taste is characterized by great finesse and roundness and a very balanced and appetizing dryness. The vine yields very grudgingly and the wine is accordingly expensive; in California, as in France, it is also used in Champagne. Perhaps two out of every three Chardonnays of the first rank that we have found have come from Napa-Sonoma wineries, but fortunately no single region has a monopoly. It should only escort foods of gourmet quality and is especially good with lobster or cracked crab and seafood generally. It can even be used as the one wine with a carefully planned buffet, for we have found it enhances chicken, turkey, cold meats, lamb and even ham when you're in the mood for something white, excellent and chilled.

Chardonnay suffers when blended very much, so it is important to look for the words "estate-bottled" or a vintage year. Christian Brothers is among the least expensive and most consistent of our favorites. Its faintly oaked style and $5 price tag contrast sharply with the almost overwhelming oak, body and varietal character of the '77 Martin Ray priced at $17. The latter ranks with the greatest white wines we've ever smelled, drunk or heard of—but nobody can produce great Chardonnay consistently. Robert Mondavi's of 1978 is the most outstanding we've ever had from that winery, while Heitz 1977 is the poorest we remember from his. The wineries besides these that we count on for unforgettable Chardonnays are Keenan, Château St. Jean, Hacienda, Château Montelena, Freemark Abbey, Mayacamas, Sterling, Stag's Leap and Z-D—most of them, alas in the $9 to $10 range. Just what they can be, at best, was demonstrated at a now-notorious Paris blind tasting where Montelena 1973 outranked the most revered of its French cousins, Le Montrachet itself.

The vintners' luck or our own has been less consistent with our second-echelon favorites: Beringer, Burgess Cellars, Charles Krug, Chappellet, Mirassou, Inglenook, Sonoma Vineyards, Simi, Trefethen and Wente Brothers. Wente's is always a rare wine of some finesse, and Mirassou's "Harvest" bottlings are often distinguished. Sonoma Vineyards' is one that seems to have improved most dramatically and Inglenook's has been the least consistent. Only an extreme strictness has enabled us to pare these listings to near-manageable proportions, be it noted, for our cellar books abound with good words for many others. Stony Hill, Hanzell, David Bruce and Chalone have also produced great Chardonnays most years, but in such limited quantity there's seldom enough for everybody who hears about it to have one good gulp apiece. We never know how we feel about Cuvaison and Fetzer; as for Dry Creek, Husch, Trentadue and Veedercrest, with some exceptional wines alternating with some mediocrities, it'll be a few years more of trial and error for all of us before we know where they rank. Chardonnay ages beautifully, by the way. We remember one from Buena Vista that was nearly nine years old and very much at its peak.

PINOT BLANC
[Pee-no' Blon]

Pinot Blanc is considered one of Chardonnay's poor cousins since it is also a white Burgundy grape. Their mutual relation, the white Gamay or Aligoté grape, is apparently neglected altogether in California. Pinot Blanc itself is more often used in the *cuvée* for Champagne or for blending purposes than sold under its own name. This is rather a mystery, for it shares considerable honors with Chardonnay on their native soil—Chassagne-Montrachet, for example, is all or mostly Pinot Blanc as a rule. Fetzer and Chalone make theirs very much in this white Burgundy tradition of subtlety and oak. Mirassou has gone so far as to call theirs "White Burgundy"; it is mostly Pinot Blanc, dry and oaky. (This wine is now a best seller whereas called by its own name, their Pinot Blanc had hardly sold at all.) Less expensive are the Pinot Blancs of Almadén, Paul Masson and Wente, wherein the taste of the grape is left free of woody flavors. Wente's in particular has a bitterish undertone that seems to make its taste just that much cleaner and crisper and complicates its fruity bouquet. Bargetto has a prize-winning example available so far only at the winery. And in the Jesuitical hands of the Novitiate of Los Gatos Pinot Blanc becomes a delicate and ever-so-slightly sweet wine most years.

All these and any others you may track down share in common a certain refreshing softness you'll never meet in a really full-bodied Chardonnay. It's probably on account of this softness that they age gracelessly and should be drunk within a year or two of bottling. A really good Pinot Blanc is most companionable with shellfish, we maintain, but will go well with fish and chicken and white meats, too. In fact, it will be an admirable but subtle buttress to them.

Sauvignon Blanc can make wines as wonderfully sweet as the great soprano chorus in Mozart's *Requiem,* but a wine of any sweetness whatever has to mind its manners impeccably for us to find it agreeable. Beaulieu's does. It is blended with some Muscadelle de Bordelais and has acid strong enough to balance its intense sugar. The only other we unreservedly recommend for subtly sweet richness and freshness combined is Château Wente, which has some Semillon added. Thankfully, Sauvignon Blancs are usually on the dry side, but you must buy them very selectively since both quality and degree of semi-sweetness vary enormously.

This is a truly noble grape whose full potential is revealed only in wine which delicately embodies contradictory qualities. It must be as dry as possible, yet still display Sauvignon's "indigenous sweetness" and fruit in taste and aroma. It must be strong in acid while giving an overall impression of softness. To be outstanding it must also be big and rich and leave a positively splendid aftertaste. The Concannons are deservedly famous for their sensitive response to this challenge Sauvignon Blanc represents, but

SAUVIGNON BLANC AND FUMÉ BLANC
[So-vee-nyon' Blon]
[Foo-may' Blon]

Dry Creek and Wente's dry version (also a damn good value) regularly surpass them in the dryness department.

Our favorite versions of this dark horse among California's choice varietals come from lesser known wineries. That from Roudon-Smith Vineyards in Santa Cruz is in such short supply as to remain mythical, perhaps; the discerning already know where to go for Spring Mountain and Sterling. Spring Mountain is invariably a dry wine of pachyderm proportions and awe-inspiring aftertaste. It is made rather in the style of white Graves (itself two-thirds Sauvignon Blanc) but with cleaner, more forceful flavors and stronger acid. We consider their '76 among the very greatest examples of this wine we've ever tasted, the '78 merely fine.

There is something marvelously Dickensian about the story of this grape, by the way, for it was something of a foundling in the Sixties, even while other grapes were being planted as fast as the ground could be prepared to receive them. Acreage devoted to it declined, in fact. But, like the hero of a Dickens story, it was suddenly shoved into the limelight, where its true nature and rightful rewards long due could be revealed.

Almost fifteen years ago Bob Mondavi produced California's first Fumé Blanc and his example woke vintners up to the fact that Sauvignon Blanc is not a principal grape in Sauternes and Graves alone. Before travelling anywhere in Europe, Papa Hemingway used to load his car trunk with his favorite white, Sancerre—ye Sauvignon Blanc tough-style. Once Americans in general acquired the taste, they proceeded to create a shortage of Sancerre and fine Pouilly-Fumé like de LaDoucette, to cite the best example only. Sancerre and Pouilly-Fumé are downright flinty wines from the Loire Valley. This is what Mr. Mondavi decided to make his Sauvignon Blanc resemble.

Now, Davis Bynum, Fetzer, Beringer and Château St. Jean have Fumé Blanc of their own. Almadén's new and improved version is also so christened, as is the Christian Brothers' clean, fresh one. Charles Krug once came out with a "Pouilly-Fumé," but was soon hooted back down to standard nomenclature. Around Pouilly-sur-Loire the Sauvignon Blanc is called Fumé Blanc, supposedly Fumé being the word for smoked and referring not—as vulgar error hath it—to the wine's taste but to the appearance of the grapes. Now one has to arch both brows at a California wine called Pouilly-Fumé, but in fact it is a re-creation of the classic type, so probably it should be called Fumé something. At least there's no danger of Fumé whatever becoming another meaningless generic term like "Sauterne." It applies only to Sauvignon Blanc made in this particular style.

We've found all the Fumés mentioned above to be fine wines and superior Sauvignon Blancs. The different vineyard selections of Château St. Jean all set a high standard, if also a trifle pricey one. All the rest offer at least intriguing variations on a more than worthy theme. Others of note are Callaway, whose '78 finally realized the promise of its cool pocket in Southern California; Parducci, whose slightly spritzy version is a different drummer that still keeps good time; and the Gallos', perhaps one of the better varietal bargains around—muted, but still very much in tune, and reducing Taylor California Cellars' effort to the acidulous *parvenu* status it deserves. Fumé Blanc will usually outperform Chardonnay on any fish course and always leaves a rainbow across the back of your tongue.

There are both sweet and dry wines from this aristocratic Bordeaux vine which is the chief ingredient of Sauternes. There are only two dry

Semillons and both come from the Livermore Valley—the Concannon and
Wente places, to be exact. This is a contention we're prepared to uphold
even against the winemasters responsible for all the others we've ever tasted;
they were fine enough in their way, but the soil of the Livermore Valley,
which only a grapevine could love, consistently produces the finest.

SEMILLON
[Say-me-yohn']

Dry Semillon can have the haunting beauty of a flute heard over still
waters. It is not great wine, certainly, but it nearly is, and that at well under
five dollars the bottle. Gowned in a color like light golden flesh, its taste,
like the aroma, is sturdy but intricate and somehow suggestive of woods'
earth. It profits from a couple years or more aging in the bottle and may be
called up for service any time you feel like an exceptional white. Excluding
Champagne, there is no better choice than Semillon to serve at brunch or
with any egg dish, for the wine's richness balances perfectly with eggs
Benedict or an omelette.

Acreage devoted to Semillon hasn't grown over the years, as other
varieties have proven more popular, perhaps because their flavors are more
direct, perhaps because comparisons with their storied European counterparts are easier. But now there is a movement afoot in California to bring
that into line, as sweet versions, naturally enriched by the noble *botrytis*,
have been made in small batches. None will yet make you think of
Sauternes, but perhaps someday they will. Most notable so far has been
Robert Mondavi, who hasn't found one good enough to release yet; in
Monterey County, there is a goodly amount of Semillon, and they usually
get *botrytis.* So there is hope.

145

JOHANNISBERG
RIESLING
*[Yo-hahn'-iss-bearg
Rees'-ling]*

Johannisberg means the "Hill of St. John," a castle-crowned mountain in Germany's Rheingau which Charlemagne is said to have selected as a site for a vineyard. However that may be, it is fairly certain that the Romans had put it to that same use centuries before his time. It was acquired during the French Revolution by William, Prince of Orange. Napoleon confiscated the vineyard after the battle of Jena and made a present of it to one of his marshals named, appropriately enough, Kellermann. Following Waterloo, the Emperor of Austria confiscated it back again and gave it to his great Chancellor, Prince von Metternich, whose descendants have owned it ever since. Dr. Kissinger does not, however, favor their wine.

The white Riesling grape responsible for all the great Rhine and Moselle wines and found in Alsace and elsewhere attains the peak of its perfection in the vineyards of Schloss Johannisberg, and it is no discredit to the Hill of St. John that California's wineries have almost unanimously adopted its name for their white Riesling wines. Johannisberg Riesling does not repudiate its German virtues in California though it produces a markedly different wine: fresh, fruity, crisply acidic and neither sweet nor dry. Its rich flavor is complemented by a pronounced flowery aroma and a silken, long-lingering aftertaste.

Any wine with so much going for it has to be complex, and the problem California vintners wrestled with for years was that most of theirs were just too simple. In 1978 Phelps, Monterey Vineyards and Rutherford Hill all came through as floral and perfectly rounded, balanced wines. These are accomplishments no vintner can repeat at will, however, for such delicate balance between sugar (or indigenous sweetness) and acid is ideally struck only in certain years. For example, Jekel managed it beautifully with their debut 1977, then somehow missed with the next vintage.

So what, then, have we a right to expect from Johannisberg Riesling on the average? Those finished to retain considerable residual sweetness, as Llords & Elwood's are, make pleasant companions only on the right occasions. Thoroughly dry ones, like the excellent 1979 Giumarra and Louis Martini's typical vintages, can be delightfully fine white wines. Both sorts are thoroughly Californian, nonetheless, with only occasional resemblances to their Rhine-grown kin. Even at their sweetest, fine German Rieslings boast an incomparable, poetic lightness that the grape has rarely displayed in its New World home, a pronouncement we offer in reverent memory of the finest from here we've ever quaffed. "Forceful" is the first word that comes to mind in describing the 1978 Landmark and '78 Château St. Jean's "Alexander Valley" version, though one would hasten to add elegant and then proceed to further ravings. Landmark's is big and powerful and fruity and bouqueted like a field of wild flowers in the noonday sun, and has terrific body. The Château St. Jean is a crisply delicate and fresh result of cold fermentation and is without wood. Both attain that ideal balance, refinement and complexity formerly so rare in Californian Rieslings, but which is becoming more common these days, thanks to a change in the minimum alcohol requirement that allows these beauties to slip below ten percent, bringing them into line with their German cousins. Even on the average, most versions you'll see these days aren't more than eleven percent alcohol, allowing the flavor to dance across your palate less encumbered.

A Napa winery that consistently does well with this variety is Stag's Leap Wine Cellars, with two separate bottlings of it well worth their price tags. Burgess (rich), Charles Krug, Concannon, Novitiate (sheer delight), J. Lohr, Simi (very delicate), Sonoma, Firestone and Wente (especially fragrant) are ten more names that cannot be forgotten as you muse over the best Rieslings ever to accompany cracked crab. Their 1978's all, in our opinion, outclass any white except top-ranking Chardonnays and Sauvignon Blancs. Each has its fresh particularity of difference, but none has sweetness you need be warned against. It would be dereliction of duty not to recommend you simply drink the lot of them.

RIESLING
LATE PICKINGS

The finest German Rieslings are emphatically not wines meant to escort the fish course, being luscious and sweet as possible. An ounce of sugar to the bottle is not unusual with these, and we seem to recollect the heaviest wine of the sort on record had several pounds, though revulsion must have made us mislay our notes on the matter. It would have been a *Trockenbeerenauslese,* that one, a wine produced from individually selected berries, just as *Auslese* is made from individually selected bunches, and *Spätlese* from the late-picked. Our glossary will define these terms in full Teutonic detail; we bring them up only as background to an historic turn of recent events in California winedom. Wines so designated have an unusually luscious subtlety imparted by the "noble rot" or, giving Latinity its due, *Botrytis cinerea,* an unappetizing-looking fungus that thrives in the Tokay, Rhine and Sauternes districts on grapes that have been allowed to overripen. Busy as He is, God has finally gotten around to introducing this beneficent pest to California and with it a new frontier of excellence where Johannisberg Riesling is concerned: Californian *Auslese* or *Spätlese* wines! Treat them as dessert, occasional or even conversation piece wines but do not miss them even if you have to pay bribery, given the short supply. They are sweet the way you find an apple sweet without being aware of its sugar; they are soft and clean-tasting as country air. The first-time-ever such release was 2,000 cases of Sonoma Vineyards' 1972 J/R Spätlese; its 10.4 percent alcohol

makes it sound comparable to a light and soft German creation, but in taste it is as Californian as its brethren be. Wente Brothers, Château Montelena and Beaulieu also produced 1972 vintaged *Aus-oder Spät-lese* Rieslings and in 1973 Beringer and Veedercrest followed suit. Each of them was unique and demonstrably worth its price.

Since then, a rush has been on; if climatic conditions weren't right for the development of *botrytis,* then the winemakers helped it along. Myron Nightingale, who created the first hand-inoculated botrytised Semillon back in 1940, fooled the grapes a few years back with overhead water sprinklers in the evenings and gave the world "Traubengold." Others just leave the grapes on the vines that much longer and pray a lot. Among those who shed no tears over answered prayers in 1978 were Callaway, Chappellet, Freemark Abbey ("Sweet Select," and it is both), Hoffman Mountain Ranch, Robert Mondavi and Joseph Phelps, which in some years rivals Château St. Jean in its variety of bottlings of the same type of grape in different categories. All these will tantalize you into sip after sip as you try to define a taste like no other you've experienced, a beauty that's its "own excuse for being."

The IRS, which controls wine labelling, now has ruled that German terms are properly reserved for German wines alone and will just confuse consumers if applied to Californian wines. Those we produce from now on must carry English designations like "Late Harvest" or "Special Picking." (Look for a sugar rating on many of them; from four to ten percent is best.) We've no quarrel with purism *über alles* in these matters. California's first (and only) *Spätlese* and *Auslese* Johannisberg Rieslings are already memorialized in our cellar books—with proof that we enjoyed them hugely.

Germany's "second" grape is supposed (by the French) to have originated somewhere in Germany or Austria. The Germans call it the Franken Riesling, however, and ascribe its origin to Alsace, where it is most widely cultivated. One of our fondest memories involves a bottle of Beaulieu's 1967 Sylvaner, but the wines one remembers best are by no means always great ones and this variety seldom makes pretentions to greatness in California. Some think it's not even a fine wine all that often, but it can be a damned good one: pale and light, crisp and smooth on the tongue. It is a thirst-quencher par excellence. Let us hope that quantities of it have been planted in Mendocino, where Parducci's comes from. Their prize-winning patch of this varietal showed to best advantage, we think, with the 1972: It had a nose like a forest in springtime and an aftertaste like stars dancing on the roof of your mouth! Though we've never had another quite as fine as that one, we're particularly fond of Beaulieu and Buena Vista Sylvaner and think Inglenook and Sebastiani also do well by the grape. These are all good or very good wines and under the right circumstances may seem fine indeed! Mirassou's popular "Monterey Riesling" is also a Sylvaner, but not one we would compare with any of the above. There are at least this many more we could enumerate, labeled now as plain "Riesling," but since none of our lists lay claim to completeness, we'll leave them for you to discover.

Gewürz is the German word for spicy, but this variety seems to shed most of its spiciness when it left its native Alsace. Californian Gewürztraminer is pleasantly soft but only mildly perfumed as compared with the Alsatian product. All the same its aroma is unusually flowery, herbaceous and delicate. (Its cousin the Traminer has the same characteristics, but they

SYLVANER
RIESLING
*/Sill-vahn'-er
Rees'-ling/*

GEWÜRZTRAMINER
/Ge-wurts-trah-me'-ner/

are less pronounced and the wine less interesting. Charles Krug and Ingle-nook produce the only Traminers we've tried.)

A Simi Gewürztraminer like their '75 or heavenly '76 is the best possible introduction to the particularly pleasant heights this grape attains. Its sweetness becomes fully apparent only after you've swallowed—and balances perfectly all the way down. In every respect as delicate as any wine can hope to be, this is what we believe all God's Gewürztraminers want to be like, and those that come anywhere close rank among California's finest whites. The Mirassous consider theirs, along with their Chenin Blanc, "closest to our standards of perfection" and the Los Angeles County Fair wine judges have several times concurred and awarded it top honors.

Grand Cru Vineyards, which only came into being in 1970, devotes much of its small production to Gewürztraminer and Zinfandel. Their most exciting experiment to date has been a Gewürztraminer "Pourriture noble" —one artificially infected with *botrytis* to produce a *Trockenbeerenaus-lese*-type dessert wine. It is obviously a varietal winemasters can take to their hearts, but most people haven't yet learned to pronounce its name. Wait for a warm afternoon and drink one, moderately chilled, either with fruit and cookies or all by itself. If the experience leaves you an unregenerate despiser of sweetish tendencies in your white wines it means just that much more Gewürztraminer for the rest of us. There's none too much of it from California anyway. The consistent success of Château St. Jean, Clos du Bois and Hacienda, along with Simi, suggests that Sonoma County may well be Gewürztraminer country, but the fine versions from Phelps do defend the honor of the Napa Valley quite well. Whatever, we are the eventual winners if there be a rivalry. This is a wine best drunk within a year or so of bottling.

Pleasure, said Aristotle, is perfect when the perfect organ finds its worthiest object. For many a late riser jaded with too many Champagne breakfasts, the wine worthiest of getting out of bed for was Wente Grey Riesling. Was, we say, for it is no longer the breakfast wine we knew. Its appellation is now simply "California" instead of "Livermore Valley" Grey Riesling and no doubt therein lies the explanation. Urban sprawl. Wente's original stand of this grape has probably disappeared beneath tract housing. Their new version is not at all the same and carries an unpleasantly bitter undertone besides. We turned to Charles Krug's in quest of a substitute only to discover new and disturbing tendencies toward sweetness in theirs! Korbel, which we also remembered as very good, disappeared from the market about the same time and we simply lost heart.

The true name of this un-noble French variety we're mourning is Chauché Gris, and it's not really a Riesling at all. It makes a wine somewhat short on acid and of simplest character—a "little" wine if you will, but a little wine to remember, fondly! In an effort to forget bygone favorites we've tried Cresta Blanca and Sonoma of late. Both are somewhat dry and refreshing but still overly unpretentious. There is little to recommend any one of them over the others. We know it *can* be a non-nondescript wine; the search continues.

This is a hybrid of Johannisberg Riesling and Muscadelle de Bordelais, developed by Professor Harold Olmo at UC Davis and introduced in 1946. Nearly 3,000 acres have been planted to it in California over the years since then, mostly in the state's hot interior valleys for which it was bred. It makes a "little" wine, medium dry and pleasing to many, but hardly fine. Paul Masson's inaccurately named Emerald Dry Riesling is probably the

best known, though San Martin has been producing one equally good just as long. Delicato, Royal Host Cellars and LaMont are also reliable brands available. Wisconsin and the environs of Lodi, California, are the only places you'll ever taste the version East-Side Winery produces. It is bone-dry and exhibits all the character Dr. Olmo could have wished for from his new varietal. We were introduced to it as the accompaniment to a fondue and for this purpose, at least, it is the perfect wine.

CHENIN BLANC
[Sheh-ne' Blon]

Chenin Blanc is the grape which produces the lovely Vouvray in the central Loire Valley, wherefore it is sometimes called the Pineau de la Loire. California Chenin Blanc is no less lovely and the best ones every year are indubitably among her finest whites. It is a wine which can call up those lines of Swinburne's

Eyes coloured like a water-flower
and deeper than the green sea's glass . . . .

It alternately takes on light-yellow or green tints and can look almost perfectly clear, like water itself. This is the California wine we've found to vary most noticeably from year to year, especially now that vintners have begun demanding more of it than simply a soft, sweetish wine. Sometime in pre-history Charles Krug became the first to bottle it as a varietal and Chenin Blancs you'd mention in the same breath with Krug's have been rare ever since. Always zesty, fresh and fruity, its sweetness and elegance will nevertheless vary from batch to batch. (Being one of Krug's non-vintaged wines, bottling dates can be especially useful here. Just look at the first six of the seven digits on the back label.) Besides Krug's the finest we know to count on are the splendid Chenin Blancs from Mirassou—foremost and first! Raymond Vineyards is worth seeking out, Kenwood is unforgettable at best. And Parducci! A good vintage from any one of them will be a rich, mouth-filling wine with marvelous aroma and perfect balance. Unlike Krug's, these are always vintage-dated so that you have the pleasure of deciding for yourself which vintner had the most luck with this varietal each year. No doubt this list of the most consistently outstanding could be lengthened, but it would take a full-time Chenin Blanc drinker to do it. Forty-odd new exemplars have come on the market since this book originally appeared.

Some of the recent arrivals are being made in a surprisingly dry style. For years the driest Chenin Blancs we tasted came from Charles Krug and Inglenook and were called, for reasons we never fathomed, White Pinot. They have been left behind on this score by a number of adventuresome winemakers taking advantage of cold fermentation, which preserves the fruitiness of the wine while it is fermented to greater dryness. Among the exemplars are Callaway, Chappellet, Dry Creek, Stags' Leap Winery and Sterling. Hacienda just entered the lists with a crisp '79 from the cool Sacramento Delta area, and if that is a sure source of supply for them, they will stand in the first rank for a long time. It should be noted that, in whatever style, these are wines meant for fairly immediate sipping.

Beringer, Christian Brothers, Simi, Woodside Vineyards (when you can find it) and Concannon are the best we remember among the lighter versions of Chenin Blancs worthy of note. Only a lover of sugary whites could recommend Christian Brothers' Pineau de la Loire; your dentist would surely advise against it.

Top-rate Chenin Blanc will always be tremendously aromatic, but we can no longer claim some residual sweetness is necessary if the varietal is to exhibit its characteristic flavor. As with Sauvignon Blanc, experimentation has revealed this grape to be much more delicate and versatile than hitherto expected in California. The more luscious have always been perfect partners with fresh fruit but, sweetish or dry, it is in combination with the alligator pear that Chenin Blanc has no peer. The smoothness of this wine together with avocado makes this simplest of luncheons memorable.

Flora, the most delicate of Dr. Olmo's creations, was first bottled in 1966, if memory serves, by Souverain's Lee Stewart. The few wineries producing it have a rather small combined production so that Flora is one of the world's rarest whites at this point, but it is one for which we predict great popularity in the future. The 1970 Parducci, our first Flora cellar book entry, recounts "Surprise! A sweet 'n sour combination unlike any other! Light body, excellent acid and balance. Only mildly scented but beautifully made wine—fine, at least." The Souverain we tried subsequently had an additional tinge of sweetness reminiscent of some Moselles. Its flowery nose we attributed to one of Flora's distinguished parents, the Gewürztraminer. (Bordeaux's Semillon is the other.) The wine is now available from tiny Robert Pecota Winery in the Napa Valley in its best-ever incarnation.

FLORA

Varietal French Colombard was almost as hard to get as Flora, til the white-wine boom and varietal tendencies drove it out of the closet. It's "Colombier" in its native Charenton Valley, where it's combined with Folle Blanche for Cognac. It was introduced into California around 1860 under the euphonious title "West's White Prolific," a nod in the direction of its six to eight tons per acre productiveness. This is the reason it remains Califor-

FRENCH COLOMBARD

nia's most widely grown white grape, but it has been relegated to the blend for Chablis and poorer grade Champagnes till of late.

Now some wineries feel they've found places to raise Colombard that's distinctive enough to stand on its own. In the northernmost and coolest parts of California we can best see its special individuality. It is fruity and crisp without the high tone of the white Burgundy types or the perfuminess of the Riesling group, its sharpness counterbalanced by good body and a pleasantly wild aroma. The examples we've found most outstanding and answering best to this description come from Cresta Blanca and Parducci in Mendocino, then Souverain, Sonoma Vineyards and Richard Carey. Davis Bynum, whose reputation makes you wish his wines weren't so unlocatable, even produced a botrytised version once that makes many a nobler grape taste bland. Giumarra and LaMont make the best we've drunk from the warmer regions.

FOLLE BLANCHE
[Fohl Blonsch]

"Crazy White" is the grape from which Cognac is made. So far as we know the only California winery producing it as a varietal is Louis M. Martini. We've found it very tart and acidic but otherwise unremarkable.

SAUVIGNON VERT
[So-vee-nyon' Vair]

This is an obscure white grape, apparently from Bordeaux. Mr. Lyle Bongé of Biloxi, Mississippi, introduced it to us as the ideal wine to accompany Gulf Coast seafood. He claims to get his supply from the very small and quality-conscious Leo Trentadue winery in Sonoma. Having never found the Trentadue (or any other) available except *chez* Bongé, we conclude the wine is undeniably a rarity, therefore, and the especially curious are invited to write for Mr. Bongé's address.

Green Hungarian is found only in California. Like the Zinfandel, its lineage is obscure, not to say unknown. It's been handed down that the first grower of this grape opined, "The less Green Hungarian there is, the better it will be." It makes a very pleasant "little" wine that is usually dry but better when it retains traces of sweetness. And, yes, you may detect a greenish cast to its color. A number of wineries use it in their blends for Rhine wine and Chablis and a handful bottle it as a varietal. This is not a noble grape, but the wine it produces has its own distinct charm and few regret making its acquaintance, particularly over a light luncheon. Sebastiani has always, in our opinion, produced the best Green Hungarian; the only others we've ever found to equal theirs came from Buena Vista. Cresta Blanca, Pedrizzetti and Weibel also offer wines of this type which are very creditable when they are not callow.

GREEN HUNGARIAN

Interesting, is it not, that Haraszthy, Green Hungarian and Zinfandel are all *said* to be from Hungary?

Malvasia is said to have originated in Greece and thence spread to southernmost Italy. God only knows what brought it to California. It is a most unusual dessert Muscat, deep golden colored, slightly bitter and intensely sweet both at once. Very much an acquired taste and one we can go long periods without missing. Others cannot. They swear Beringer and San Martin make the finest in the hemisphere.

MALVASIA BIANCA
[Maal-vah-see'-ah Bee-ank'-kah]

ROSÉ   Rosé is always refreshing to drink and ever so pleasing to look at; it is an all-purpose wine that never clashes with a menu. The fact that Mateus' and Lancer's Portugese rosés are such top-selling imports in these United States—and that at ridiculous prices—attests to our national naiveté in matters vinous. At the same time, it shows that rosé is the easiest wine for non-wine drinkers to enjoy. Even varietal rosés are not expected to be terribly distinctive or truly fine, but this doesn't keep them from being delicious. Most of the better European and Californian rosés are made from the Grenache grape. (Almadén's is one of the better Grenache rosés available.) The rosés which Gamay and Zinfandel yield are even better yet. Beringer and Robert Mondavi both have very spritely Gamays, but our favorites are Concannon's and Pedroncelli's Zinfandel. Something new is Pinot Noir rosé, and among the better versions thereof are Simi and Buena Vista. All are pleasant companions with a light lunch.

Grignolino rosé is a startling orange hue and very pleasant likewise. We can recommend Heitz Cellars'. Though on the less dry side, some of the most distinguished pink wines we can recollect were made from Cabernet Sauvignon by Buena Vista, Llords & Elwood and Simi. At the peak of the pack is the delightful rosé originally made by mistake by the Mirassous; they call it Petite Rosé from the Petite Sirah that goes into it.

Rosé wines may be light or dark pink, medium or bone-dry. They profit not at all from bottle aging—the younger they are drunk the better they seem to be. Practically every winery has a rosé on the market and we've never encountered one truly offensive. These few we've noted, however, are the only examples that don't taste to us like sheep in sheep's clothing.

CABERNET
SAUVIGNON
*[Kabear-nay'
So-vee-nyon']*

This is at best a wine to accompany an hour of Mozart or Pergolese. Its character, like their music, is both strong and delicate, infinitely rich in nuance yet completely balanced and harmonious. Cabernet Sauvignon usually starts off a deep ruby color which takes on a tinge of orange with age. Though you will find Cabernets of every consistency, the best seem to be neither slender nor especially powerful in build but medium-bodied, in between. As wine writers never tire of repeating, this is the principal grape producing the master wines of Bordeaux: Lafite-Rothschild, Margaux, Latour, Haut-Brion, Mouton-Rothschild and all those other nobles whose company these keep. In California it has been acknowledged the most extraordinary of her fine reds (till of late, when Zinfandel developed new dimensions and entered the rivalry). Most of the best comes from Napa/Sonoma, though other areas come close in good years.

In France Cabernet is always blended, but the best Californian Cabernets are either blended very little—usually then with Merlot—or else not blended at all. What results is a wine that in some respects out-Clarets Bordeaux: in flavor generally more forceful and less complex, but just as warm and richly scented. Like Bordeaux, Cabernet should *never* be drunk immediately. It starts out full of tannin and therefore astringent as anything can be, rough and hard. Only time can transmute such wine into elixir, and the best may continue to improve for fifteen or twenty years if given a good home. Admittedly it's already drinkable by the age of four or five, but by the time it's seven or eight that same wine is something else indeed, and well worth waiting for. The reasonably priced and very special Sebastiani Special Bottlings have shown the truth of this statement; they're never released until they approach their peak of drinkability. (If all this makes you want to lay away a few cases each year, you'll discover it's possible to arrange here on earth for certain of those rewards which are in heaven.)

Vintage variations between Cabernets are always noticeable. Napa Valley being California's premiere growing region, it is not amiss to compare the seasons '73 through '78. This collation of comments is from Beaulieu's Legh Knowles, Frank Wood of Freemark Abbey and others of the Napa Valley brotherhood.

- *1973* Most copious harvest of the decade and excellent in quality.
- *1974* Late year. Cool summer and fall, warming finally coming in October. Another large crop of exceptional quality. Wines of tremendous potential, perhaps the vintage of the decade.
- *1975* A very late harvest, the slow ripening insuring deep full varietal character and high fruit acid. Large yield and rather flavorful reds (and whites) predicted—though with some reservations at this point.
- *1976* First year of the drought led to some dehydration of the grapes and a smaller crop therefore, but also to a concentration of flavor and character. The wines will be noted more for power than finesse, and should be aged at least ten years.
- *1977* Second year of drought, but this time the vintners were prepared and pruned the vines to ease their strain, providing a better balance to many of the wines. Slightly lower in alcohol than the usual California average, which may enhance the flavors.
- *1978* Heat waves in the fall raised grape sugars before the grapes fully ripened, then came sporadic rains; for this vintage, as well as that of 1979, which was uneven in a different way, the prognosis is guarded optimism.

Microclimatical exceptions abound, but this will roughly characterize a great many notable Napa Valley Cabernets, some of which we'll still be drinking ten years from now.

Elsewhere we've described new-style Cabernets that qualify as some of the greatest we remember. Those of equal stature almost always include: Beaulieu's Georges de Latour Private Reserve, Charles Krug's vintage selections, Inglenook cask bottlings, Heitz Cellars, Mayacamas and Robert Mondavi. These are about the only ones we pay for by reflex and without further thought. Invariably expensive, but also among the world's greatest reds. There's no easy way of finding Californian Cabernets that equal them each year, though many are produced. The classic 1974 Heitz Martha's Vineyard is still not $15 better than the 1977 Clos du Val, for instance. As for Cabernets for less, Louis Martini's are hard to surpass.

At this point we must leave you to the good offices of your wine merchant. Too much good news is bad for purposes of clear exposition, and the market has been glutted with Cabernet Sauvignons of the first rank. What's the point in recommending the 1976 Jordan or 1977 Burgess, Stag's Leap or Villa Mt. Eden? They also have a rightful place beside the world's greatest, but there's no guaranteeing you can find them. Nor is there any way of knowing when subsequent vintages will measure up. Even Almadén won gold medals for its 1977, a bargain; the state of the art is just fine enough of the time, it seems. Discovering the best in your locale is up to you. We can't guarantee that a bottle from any of these will be truly great, but any sensitive merchant can guide you to one that, in the words of the fine poet Jack Gilbert ". . . is the normal excellence, of long accomplishment."

Cabernet Sauvignon seems to us lamb's ideal accomplice, though many may disagree with this preference. Like the music of a Mozart, you can always savor it just for its own sweet sake.

Merlot is a not-so-minor black grape whose cultivation Louis Martini pioneered in California. In the Bordeaux country it's nearly as important as the two Cabernets, being an essential ingredient in the blend for nearly all the great Clarets. The fine wines of Pomerol and St. Emilion are sometimes, like Château Petrus, made exclusively from Merlot. Martini's Merlot certainly qualifies as some of the softest, roundest and most agreeable red California now produces. Using the *maceration carbonique* method (whereby the grape juice ferments while still inside the grapes!) Sterling Vineyards once produced a peculiar Merlot Primeur. Though definitely not a wine for every palate, the Lord will forgive them their experiments, for they know what they are after. In the case of their straight Merlot, Sterling has already found it. Gundlach-Bundschu and Rutherford Hill are also coming up fast. Phelps' "Insignia" has a fair amount of Cabernet blended into it, and aims to challenge Petrus someday.

MERLOT
[Mair-low']

A cross between Bordeaux's Cabernet Sauvignon and the Carignane of Southern France and Algeria, Ruby Cabernet was intended to retain Cabernet's aroma—poorly described as "green olive" by the scientists—while withstanding, Carignane-like, high temperatures that would cripple Cabernet. The actual result has been an invertebrate wine that usually deserves Mr. Churchill's reaction to the pudding. ("Waiter, pray remove this pudding—it has no theme.") The first of any note came, we understand, from the quality-minded, Port-producing Ficklin vineyards in the hottest part of the San Joaquin Valley. The vast majority of the 10,000 acres plus now coming into bearing is found in regions of similar climate, the best of it so far being that of LaMont. Ruby Cabernets from Fortino and San Martin are also worth their prices in our opinion.

RUBY CABERNET

Marching past Burgundy's Clos de Vouget, one of Napoleon's colonels called his men to attention and ordered them to present arms to the vineyard. *"Mes braves,"* he is reported to have said, "it is to defend beauties like these that you are called upon to fight." The great grape of that vineyard is the Pinot Noir. Burgundies which attain a greatness of their own comparable to the greatest Clarets are rare in France. California Pinot Noirs equal to the best Cabernet Sauvignon do not exist . . . or so we used to say. But Stonegate Napa Valley 1976 now—there is a burgundy, by God—a Pinot Noir *in excelsis!* Addicts of this grape's masculine glamor pray for a wine like this, "that kisses, licks, bites, thrusts and stings" as Michelangelo the younger once put it. We want it rich, full-bodied and velvety, with an aggressive savoriness and the color of the wine dark sea.

PINOT NOIR
[Pee-no' Nwor]

To find such you do a lot of tasting or else take your wine merchant's advice. Nowadays there are California Pinot Noirs that will live up to these expectations, but they're just as rare as first-rate Cabernets are plentiful. Most of us will have to accept on faith the very real glories of Joseph Swan's, for instance, since his winery's total production is never likely to exceed 3,000 cases. We should also mention here that most California Pinot Noirs are consumed much too early; because they tend to be lighter than true Burgundies, people gulp them right down. To be truest to thine own self, try holding on to some for five years or so. A wondrous bouquet and character will develop, a softness that is very much in line with the Nuits-St.-Georges tradition—and in the tradition of Napa's greatest Pinot Noirs as well. These come, when at all, from Beaulieu ("Carneros" 1976), Burgess, Caymus, Martini and Robert Mondavi. It frequently happens that all of them are a shade *too* light bodied, which is our chief complaint against the Joseph Phelps 1978 we just tried; ordinarily his are among the best bets also. Many

'75's and '76's are true *aristos* and ready for drinking soon; certain '77's—Robert Mondavi's notably—will taste even better. Fine Pinot Noirs from these years will profit enormously from more time spent in the bottle, at least five years and perhaps more. With that proviso, Spring Mountain and Z D 77's should provide awesome peak experiences with this wine, for example. Many of these mentioned are grown in Napa's Carneros Creek district, by the way, where the new Carneros Creek Winery is also producing some outrageously superb examples.

Fortunately Napa has no monopoly. Sonomas's Pedroncelli has the most reliable record of all in producing Pinot Noir of the first rank; it is also some of the least expensive. Kenwood did very well in 1976 and offers a '77 "Jack London Vineyard" that is simply wonderful. Fetzer always merits high marks and Sonoma Vineyards can also deserve honest praise—but what is there to say for Mirassou and Parducci? We speak of their 1974's in hushed tones for the opposite reasons: The Parducci was as rambunctious as the Mirassou was smooth, but they've not equalled these since. Their Pinot Noirs non-*extraordinaire* should perhaps be grouped with Cresta Blanca, Llords & Elwood, Foppiano, San Martin and Wente—always good but to our taste only sometimes worthy of a salute.

GAMAY AND
GAMAY
BEAUJOLAIS
[Gah-may'
Bozho-lay']

Gamay and Gamay Beaujolais are two very similar varieties. Grapes have a proclivity to "clone" incestuously and nobody today seems positive which of the two is the genuine grape of Beaujolais from the south of Burgundy. Not that it matters greatly, for the wines they produce are virtually indistinguishable in California, generally "little" with grapy aroma of no particular distinction, light bodied and light colored and with a pleasant, fruity taste. None of them have the magic of the finest French

Beaujolais (which is never plentiful), though like Beaujolais, the younger they are drunk, the better they are likely to be. They are best as picnic or lunch-time wines served with stews, chops, fried chicken, or cold meats. There are few we would serve as dinner wines, however. We prefer these reds served cooler than others.

Some thirty-five or forty wineries are currently producing Gamay or Gamay Beaujolais, but a truly fine wine by these names has always been rare in our experience. In 1974 Parducci vinted one we think better than any we've had since, probably because it was so atypically big and chewy. Accolades for the best of the typical pass back and forth between Sebastiani and Christian Brothers (whose Gamay Noir is very smooth, very fine). The luck of many other producers seems to fluctuate with this grape(s), making it impossible to distinguish favored growing regions and very difficult to come up with runner-up brands. Beaulieu's we remember fondly, and likewise that from Mirassou, Martini, Pedroncelli and Sonoma. More expensive but highly recommended are those from Robert Mondavi and Ridge (hard to find, but worth the search).

During the past several years, some wineries have followed the lead of Sebastiani in producing "Nouveaux" from these varieties. Carbonic maceration-made wines, they taste downright grapy to us, but their freshness and fruit should have a wide appeal. As with French Beaujolais Nouveau, these are released punctually on November 15th each year and are meant to be consumed soon after.

According to some authorities, this is not a true Pinot, but that need not hamper your enjoyment of it. Now that Inglenook has uprooted their old, low-yield stand (whose wine they sold as "Red Pinot") California's

PINOT ST. GEORGE
[Pee-no' Sein Zhorge]

169

solitary Pinot St. George comes from Christian Brothers. It is an all-time ideal light red, a joy to inhale and the very definition of delicious! Against the best scientific advice the Brothers have enlarged their plantings and one thanks God that they are men of faith.

PETITE SIRAH
[Puh-teat' Cyr-ah']

Petite Sirah may have been growing in the Rhône Valley north of the French Riviera back in the days when Pliny the Elder and Plutarch were singling out the wines of this region for special accolades. But tradition says it was introduced by a returning crusader, the worthy Sir Gaspard de Sterimberg. It's been thought the variety originated around Schiraz, Persia, but any etymological basis for this assumption is shaky since the grape is also known as Sirrac, Serrine and Syrrah. Though the date is variously given—1124 or 1225—it is certain that Sir Gaspard began raising it when he gave up this world for the life of a hermit at St. Christophe's on the mountain which has ever since produced one of the world's great wines, Hermitage. This "manliest of wines," as the blessed Saintsbury called it, consists mainly of Petite Sirah, which is also the backbone of our beloved Chateauneuf-du-Pape.

The grape which boasts this distinguished, if confused, pedigree also produces some of California's least known but most outstanding varietal wines. We are told that two distinct varieties are raised under this name in California. We cannot say whether we should look to this or to the way the wine is made or to the ground the grape is grown on for the differences among Petite Sirah wines that are becoming increasingly apparent.

Joseph Phelps has had some luck with a clone he claims is the true Syrah, developed from cuttings brought from the Rhône; it makes wine hard as a miser that demands ten years *en bouteille* before paying off. Robert Mondavi makes a fuller, softer version that is consistent, spicy, almost chewy; astonishingly, he may stop making it, to streamline his line. Parducci and Ridge favor a highly tannic, earthy approach also. Our '74 unfined Parducci is just beginning to turn in its best performance now that we're running out of it, and no doubt we'll also have greedily consumed all our '74 and '75 Stonegate before it's fully beatified. Certain of their other vintages have verged on greatness likewise, as will an occasional Souverain, Burgess or Trentadue Petite Sirah in this style. The Freemark Abbey version does not, like all these, near Brucean intensity—it is unique in its own right, combining woodiness and a peculiar peppery quality we've encountered in no other wine. As a poet said somewhere, it creates

> A moment of unrecapturable surprise
> As when a child first finds
> Echo speaks his language, too.

These are the least "petite" of the Petite Sirahs we know, but none of the others could possibly be considered diminutive. In 1964 the Concannons became the first to bottle it as a varietal and theirs has set a standard for quality ever since. It is usually smooth as glycerine, soft and mellow but very dry all the same. Mirassou (with variations), Mount Madonna, Pedrizzetti (especially), San Martin and Wente are further fine examples of this type as a rule. They may be harder and more tannic in some years than in others, but a pachyderm fleshiness and body typify them all at their best. The Cresta Blanca and Foppiano Petite Sirahs are the two we prize most from more northerly producers, but we've never met a Petite Sirah we didn't like. Let us hope this continues to be true when the vast new plantings of it begin to bear. New acreage is about equally divided between north

coastal and inland valley vineyards because the variety adapts much better than most to different soils and climatic conditions.

Petite Sirah seems, on the whole, most appropriate to heavier dishes —steaks, roasts and other hearty fare of the meat-and-potatoes ilk.

We regret to report that the mystery—nay, the romance—surrounding the origin of Zinfandel has begun to dissipate since our first edition. The first man to raise it, Colonel Haraszthy, never could decide where this variety came from and who sent it to California and neither has anyone since, we wrote then. Shortly thereafter, someone turned up a *Treatise on Grapes* written by New Yorker William Robert Prince twenty-two years before Haraszthy's 1852 Zinfandel planting. Prince mentions a grape he had grown under glass that came, he thought, from Hungary and that was called Zinfandel. Since Eastern nurseries supplied many of the *vinifera* vines California imported in those days, Mr. Prince's hothouse may well have been the immediate source of California's foundling. In *Wines of America* Leon Adams suggested that the grape did not come from Hungary at all but may ultimately be traced to the "Zingarello" which is raised near Taranto on the instep of Italy's boot. Hopefully time will tell us no more, but even this much is enough to leave the dashing figure of "the Father of California Viticulture," "Count" or "Colonel" Haraszthy (Adams avers he was neither), out in the historical cold. The only romantic touch in all this academic research is that "Zingarello" does translate "gypsy."

No matter its pedigree and peregrinations, Zinfandel will remain uniquely Californian, a wine without counterpart anywhere else in the world. If you discount the Carignane, no wine grape in California rivals the versatile Zinfandel in popularity and sheer quantity of production. Depend-

ZINFANDEL
[Zin'-fan-dell]

ing upon where it is grown and how vinified, it actually produces many different kinds of wine. Most everyday jug Zinfandels fall into that category of "good" wine—less than fine but undeniably better than *ordinaire*. Those of the next rank are a sort of equivalent to French Beaujolais: zesty and full of fruit and best for drinking while youthful. Our favorite examples come from Martini, Sebastiani and Foppiano ("Russian River Valley"). In exceptional years (1974 and 1976 leap to mind) they turn out as fine as sex, with a specific gravity, so to speak, that no French Beaujolais attains.

The comparison, if you insist on one, would have to be with Cabernet Sauvignon, and personally we would choose the "best" Zinfandel over most Cabernets. The best we remember also include bottles from Buena Vista, Clos du Val, Charles Krug, Kenwood, Mirassou, Parducci and Sutter Home. Any of these will represent one of the best wine values currently available. Our list is an enormously abbreviated one, though, for fine Zinfandels have become too numerous to count.

Traditional Zinfandels like this serve merely as an introduction to this grape's grand future. Dr. David Bruce, whom we must thank for the first *white* Zinfandel ever we tried, is not alone in his stated ambition "to bring the mountain-grown Zinfandel to the place it deserves in the world of fine wines." Wines as vivid as he and his co-visionaries produce have never before been seen on land or sea—deep and fiery flavored with heavy, pervasive bouquets, as much wood as grape, as full of body as Virgil, and damn near black. European-trained palates will find them hard to get used to, for wines like this come on like gangbusters. It's hard to imagine a taste so big being elegant as well, but it is, it is!

Among those boarding this bandwagon in 1976 and '77 were Carneros Creek, Burgess, Dehlinger, Monteviña, Roudon-Smith and a host of others from all over the state, swinging lustily to hit one out of the park and succeeding. If you possess the temerity to become a partisan of these monsters, there is more good news in store for you—1978 saw a heat wave during the harvest that quickly drove up the grape sugars while the acids were high, which has resulted in wines that are truly awesome—fifteen percent alcohol or so is about normal, the mouth-feel about that of a rare filet mignon, the character intense. These wines are not just aggressive, they're downright ferocious; not wines, as Rod Strong recently remarked, that you'd want to meet in a dark alley. They'll still be huge in another ten years, and might even be agreeable to anyone with that much patience.

Zinfandel has become a specialty, not to say a fetish, with Ridge, whose distinctive labels read like liner notes to symphony recordings. Their wines are expensive, but there's no better way of appreciating the vast differences among Zinfandels than setting side-by-side Ridge wines of the same vintage from different vineyards. As G. Stein observed, "You have to really love what is to have pleasure" and nothing you've drunk can prepare your palate for pleasures like those of a full-throttle Zinfandel. Open your mind and roll your eyes!

Zinfandel's untapped potential is further illustrated by Napa's Sutter Home Winery. They've decided to specialize in this varietal, and their Deaver Vineyard selections give some idea of the splendors coming from Amador County, while their experiments continually amaze. The White Zinfandel we just tasted is comparable to only one wine in the world: a highly prized white Veneto called San Osvaldo which is also made from black grapes. The resulting salmon hue accounts for the name, but in body and subtlety this Sutter Home white surpasses David Bruce's and even Grand Cru Vineyards' Zinfandel Blanc de Noir. These ideal aperitif wines are novelties still, but they already have competition. Delicious dessert wine and beautifully bright rosés (like Concannon's) have also been made from this grape. Sutter Home, Monteviña (also from Amador County) and Grand Cru Vineyards have even produced Zinfandel Nouveaux that are worthy of note. More so than any other variety, Zinfandel seems to be the ordained herald of the Golden Age of California Wine.

CARIGNANE
[Care-in-nyan']

Drinking Carignane is like rooting for the underdog. Practically no one knows its name, yet more acreage is planted to it in California than any other red, Zinfandel included. Its importance up till now has depended on the vigor and bountifulness of the vine and not the quality of its wine, which has always been used for *ordinaires* anonymous and worse. Despite this reputation, a number of wineries have found in it merits sufficient to justify bottling Carignane as a varietal. Simi, where it's something of a tradition, makes a rather soft wine of it that has good flavor and a pleasant finish. Innovative outfits like David Bruce have also had entrants in the field. Of these we most enjoyed Oakville's Grande Carignane '73, but the Carmine Carignane from Fetzer in Mendocino remains, alongside Simi's, the very favorite in our memory. It had an aftertaste like nothing you've ever experienced—and not everybody may relish. Try one if you run across it.

BARBERA
[Bar-bear'-ah]

Italian immigrants brought Barbera vines from their native Piedmont to the valleys encircling San Francisco in the mid-nineteenth century, and this varietal has remained the special province of Italian-descended winemakers down to our own time. The variety has done as well in California as ever it did in Italy, producing rugged full-bodied wines almost purple in color and often biting on the tongue. It ages well: Indeed, we've enjoyed super-mature Sebastianis whose bouquet was discernable all around the table as soon as the first glass was poured and that proved on tasting as elegant and harmonious as fine wine can hope to be. It is a grape whose excellences have been overlooked. Those from Sebastiani and Louis Martini have long been the most highly regarded, but we have recently found comparable examples from Fortino and Rapazzini. We also recommend the outstanding Barberas from Bargetto, Buena Vista, Monteviña and, particularly, Pedrizzetti.

No dish yet devised is strong enough to overpower Barbera, especially when it is young. It will stand up to garlic, anchovies, curries, barbecue and everything else the fastidious worry about serving with wine. To us, and not surprisingly, it seems best when matched with spicy Italian dishes.

Barberone means "big Barbera," a considerably rougher and coarser wine which is usually made just a touch or two sweeter and sold in bulk. We recommend the "CK" brand and Delicato.

GRIGNOLINO
[Greeg-no-lee'-no]

This grape is another native of Italy's Piedmont; in California it attains its peak in the hands of Beringer's Myron Nightingale. He makes it into a bone-dry wine of very light body, with a very strong varietal nose, medium color and a properly Italianate whiplash in the taste. Heitz and Mount Madonna (the Emilio Guglielmo prestige label) are the only others to demonstrate how distinctive Grignolino can be. Cresta Blanca and San Martin make very pleasantly scented "littler" wines from this varietal.

CHARBONO
[Shar-bo-no']

Charbono is a distinctive, rich and heavy-bodied wine produced from this Italian variety by Inglenook. Their notable success with it probably accounts for its being grown by Davis Bynum, Franciscan and Papagni of late, but we are still looking for their bottlings.

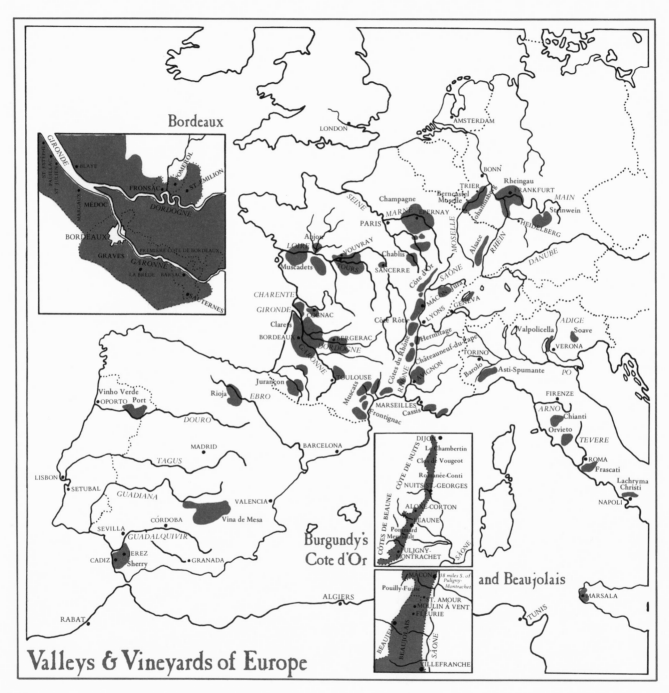

Bordeaux

GIRONDE
ST ESTÉPHE
PAUILLAC
ST JULIEN
BLAYE
MARGAUX
MÉDOC
FRONSAC
POMEROL
ST EMILION
DORDOGNE
BORDEAUX
GRAVES
PREMIÈRE CÔTE DE BORDEAUX
GARONNE
LA BRÈDE
BARSAC
SAUTERNES

Burgundy's Cote d'Or

DIJON
CÔTE DE NUITS
Le Chambertin
Clos de Vougeot
Romanée-Conti
NUITS-ST.-GEORGES
CÔTES DE BEAUNE
ALOXE-CORTON
BEAUNE
Pommard
Meursault
PULIGNY-MONTRACHET
SAÔNE

and Beaujolais

MÂCON
38 miles S. of Puligny-Montrachet
Pouilly-Fuisse
ST. AMOUR
MOULIN À VENT
BEAUJOLAIS
FLEURIE
SAÔNE
VILLEFRANCHE

LONDON
AMSTERDAM
BONN
TRIER
Berncastel
Moselle
Rheingau
FRANKFURT
Johannisberg
MAIN
Steinwein
HEIDELBERG
Alsace
RHEIN
MOSELLE
DANUBE
Champagne
MARNE
EPERNAY
SEINE
PARIS
Anjou
LOIRE
VOUVRAY
Chablis
TOURS
SANCERRE
Côte d'Or
SAÔNE
MÂCON
Jura
Côte Rôti
GENEVA
LYONS
Valpolicella
ADIGE
Soave
VERONA
Hermitage
Côtes du Rhône
Châteauneuf-du-Pape
AVIGNON
TORINO
Barolo
Asti-Spumante
PO
CHARENTE
GIRONDE
COGNAC
Clarets
BORDEAUX
BERGERAC
DORDOGNE
GARONNE
TOULOUSE
RHÔNE
Muscats
MARSEILLES
Frontignac
Cassis
FIRENZE
ARNO
Chianti
Orvieto
TEVERE
ROMA
Frascati
Lachryma Christi
NAPOLI
Jurançon
Rioja
EBRO
Vinho Verde
OPORTO
Port
DOURO
MADRID
BARCELONA
LISBON
TAGUS
SETUBAL
GUADIANA
VALENCIA
Vina de Mesa
CÓRDOBA
SEVILLA
GUADALQUIVIR
CADIZ
JEREZ
Sherry
GRANADA
ALGIERS
TUNIS
MARSALA
RABAT

Valleys & Vineyards of Europe

GLOSSARY

ACIDITY
Fixed acidity is wine's natural fruit-acid content that can only be determined by tasting. (Volatile acidity is its vinegar or acetic acid and is indetectable in good wine.) Acidity gives the wine its structure and the tartness that makes it refreshing. Insufficient acidity results in flabby, formless wine, while too much produces wine that tastes thin, sourish and unripe.

AMONTILLADO
[Ah-mont-ee-ah'-doe]
Spanish. Popular type of Sherry, very dry and unusually well aged.

APÉRITIF *[Ah-pear-ee-teef']*
French. An appetizer, usually a flavored and/or fortified wine.

APPELLATION CONTRÔLÉE
[Ah'-pell-ah-see-ohn Cawn-trol-ay']
French. Literally "controlled appellation." Words found on the label of any genuine French wine of real quality guaranteeing that it is entitled to the name it bears. The finer the wine, the more specific the designation. Names of vineyards, villages, communes, and whole districts are officially recognized and delimited. An appellation movement now is inexorably spreading across California.

ARMAGNAC *[Ar-mahn-nyack']*
Region in France near the Pyrenees which produces a splendid brandy of the same name.

AROMA
The distinctive odor of the particular grape from which the wine was made.

ASTI SPUMANTE
[Ahs-tee' Spoo-mahn'-tay]
A muscat sparkling wine from the Piedmonte region in Italy. Italian *spumanti* are of many different kinds.

ASTRINGENCY
Wines that seem to dry and pucker the mouth and feel rough on the tongue are astringent. This is usually due to excessive tannin and tends to disappear with bottle-aging.

AUSLESE *[Ows'-lay-seh]*
German. Literally "selected." The wine is from the ripest selected bunches of grapes which have the *edelfaule* or "noble rot" on them. See *edelfaule*.

BALLING
A measurement of the degree of grape sugar and therefore of ripeness. Speaking very unmathematically, about two degrees Balling in the grape translates into 1 percent alcohol in the wine. The usual 12 percent alcohol content thus comes from grapes picked at around 24 degrees Balling. Late-picked grapes may have much higher Balling.

BAROLO *[Bah-roh'-low]*
An excellent Italian red wine from the Piedmont region.

BARSAC *[Bar-sok']*
Wine from the commune of this name near the Sauternes district in Bordeaux; sweet, but generally drier than Sauternes.

BEAUNE *[Bone]*
A winemaking and marketing center for Burgundy's wines located in the Côte de Beaune (the southern section of the Côte d'Or).

BEERENAUSLESE
[Beer'-en-ows'-lay-seh]
German. Literally "berry-selected." Rich, sweet and expensive wine made from individually selected grapes which are overripe and covered with the "noble rot."

BERGERAC *[Bear'-zhair-ack']*
Bergerac wine named for the town near Bordeaux; dry reds and semi-sweet whites, both very good as a rule.

BERNCASTEL *[Burn'-kass-tell]*
Small town on the Moselle which produces very fine wines, Berncasteler Doktor being the most famous.

BLANC DE BLANC *[Blon deh Blon]*
White wine from white grapes, especially Champagnes (which are customarily made from both white and black grapes).

BOCKSBEUTEL *[Box'-boy-tell]*
German. The squat flagon in which white Steinwein from Germany and Chilean Riesling is bottled.

BODEGA *[Bo-day'-gah]*
Spanish. A winery, a wine shop or a wine producer's cellars.

BODY
The density or consistency of a wine in relation to its alcoholic strength.

BOTTLE SICKNESS
A kind of claustrophobia that besets most wines after they are first bottled and thus deprived of air, resulting in a temporary loss of flavor. It usually lasts only a few weeks but may recur in fine wines after travelling. Often fatal in such cases—caution!

BOTRYTIS CINEREA
[Bo-try'-tis ki-ner-e'-a]
The so-called "noble rot," a type of mold that flourishes on overripe grapes in the Tokay, Rhine and Sauternes districts and is responsible for their sweetest and finest whites. It was first discovered in Hungary in the 17th century and has occurred since 1972 in California also.

BOUQUET *[Boo-kay']*
French. The scent, the breath a wine gives off in the glass after it is poured. Unlike aroma, bouquet is produced by bottle aging.

BOURGOGNE *[Boor-goyn']*
French. The province of Burgundy.

BOUTIQUE
A trade term for California wineries of very small output, whence cometh a disproportionate number of her finest wines.

BREED
The total virtues of a wine, considering all the qualities associated with that type of wine.

BRIX *[Bree']*
French equivalent to Balling often substituted for the English term out of delicacy. See Balling.

CABINET (or **KABINETT**)
[Kah-be-net']
A superior grade of German wine, less sweet than any -*Lese*. This is the lowest of the six *Pradikat* (attributes) that can be claimed by the most expensive and finest German wines—*Qualität-swein mit Pradikat.*

CAVES *[Kahv]*
French. Literally "cellars," wine storehouses, aging cellars.

CHAMBERTIN *[Shawm-bear-tehn']*
Classic Burgundy red-wine vineyard, name also given to village and commune of Gevrey-Chambertin. "Le Chambertin" is the best of several Burgundies legally allowed to use this name in hyphenated form.

CHARMAT BULK PROCESS
A shortcut method of making sparkling wine invented by the Frenchman Charmat. It produces inferior bubbly.

CHIANTI *[Key-ahn'-tee]*
An Italian wine named for the League of Chianti region in central Italy's Tuscany between Florence and Siena.

CLARET
The common English name for the red wines of Bordeaux. These were originally called *vin clairet,* or "clear wine," to distinguish them from the wine which was kept in cellars to mature. *Vin clairet* was primarily used for export.

CLOS *[Klo]*
French. Literally, an enclosed yard; vineyard, usually of high repute.

COGNAC *[Ko'-nyack]*
French Brandy from the district it's named for.

COLD FERMENTATION
Use of steel-jacketed, water-cooled fermentation tanks to control the heat of the process and thus slow it down. Whites made with this technology display notably heightened acid, fruit and balance.

COMMUNE *[Koh-mewh']*
French. A parish or township.

CÔTE (-S) [Coat]
French. Literally "slope" or "hillside"; a winegrowing area.

CÔTE D'OR [Coat dohr']
A region of central Burgundy, some thirty-six miles long and less than one mile wide, where the finest Burgundies are grown.

CÔTE RÔTIE [Coat Row-tee']
A red-wine region on the Rhône near Vienne producing fine reds.

CRACKLING
Semi-sparkling, slightly fizzy. "Pétillant."

CRU [Crew]
French. Literally a "growth," a planting or crop; a vineyard or group of vineyards; wine from a specific vineyard.

CRUST
The sediment that adheres to the inside of a bottle, indicating a well-aged wine. Especially "crusted" vintage Port.

CUVÉE [Koo-vay']
French. Literally "tubful"; the blend of several wines, as for Champagne.

DESSERT WINES
Sweet wines served either with dessert or as dessert themselves, alone. Generally fortified.

DOMAINE [Doe-main']
French. Vineyard. The control or management of several vineyards.

DOSAGE [Doe-saaje']
French. The process of adding sugared wine and brandy to bottle-fermented sparkling wines before they are corked.

DOURO [Door'-roh]
A river and a wine region of central Portugal famous for Port.

D'YQUEM (CHÂTEAU) [Dee-kem']
"First growth" Sauternes, Bordeaux.

EAUX-DE-VIE [Oh-deh-vee']
French. Brandy distilled from the leavings of crushed grapes, usually raw and terrifyingly powerful. Same as *marc* or *grappa*.

EDELFAULE [Ay'-dell-fohl]
German. The so-called "noble rot" or *pourriture noble*. See *Botrytis cinerea*.

ENOLOGY
The science and study of making wine and growing grapes for wine, pioneered by Louis Pasteur; it is related to viticulture.

ESTATE-BOTTLED
Semi-official designation of a wine fermented and bottled on the specific vineyard property where the grapes were grown. California's equivalent to "château-bottled," etc.

FINESSE [Fee-ness']
French. A wine's elegance or delicacy. Also the quality of its aftertaste, the lingering scent and warmth in the throat after a wine has been swallowed.

FINISH
The characteristics of a wine that remain in the mouth and nasal passages after the wine has been swallowed; another term for aftertaste.

FINO [Fee'-no]
Spanish. A common type of Sherry, very dry and pale.

FIRMNESS
The rawness typical of young wines, mainly alcoholic in character.

FLOR [Floor]
Spanish. The yeast which is responsible for the nutty character of dry Spanish Sherries. The process is increasingly used in California.

FORTIFIED WINE
Aperitifs and dessert wines to which grape spirits (brandy) have been added.

FRAPPÉ [Frah-pay']
French. Iced or chilled.

FRASCATI [Frahs-kaht'-ee]
Best known of Italy's Castelli Romani wines grown near Rome; dry and full-bodied whites and reds.

GENERIC
Names such as Burgundy, Rhine wine, Chianti and so forth as applied to American wines. Used thus without any geographical significance, these names mean next to nothing to the consumer.

GRAND *[Grahn]*
French. Large, great or superior. Usually unofficial and meaningless.

GRAPPA *[Grah'-pah]*
Italian. Brandy. (See *marc*).

GRAVES *[Grahv]*
An important red and white wine district near Bordeaux.

HARD
Containing too much tannin, hence unpleasant. Such wines, though requiring longer aging than others, are finally tamed in the process of maturing and become excellent.

HAUT-BRION (CHÂTEAU–)
[Oh-bree-yohn']
A "First Growth" red Graves considered one of the finest of all Clarets.

HAUT-SAUTERNE *[Oh-so-tairn']*
An American term for distinguishing sweeter whites, thought to resemble the wines from the Sauternes district in France, from dry Sauterne. The name of the wine, like the name of the district, is always spelled with a final "s" in France.

JOHANNISBERG (SCHLOSS)
[Schlohs Yo-hahn'-iss-bearg]
A world-renowned vineyard on the mountain overhanging Johannisberg in Germany's Rheingau region. It has given its name to the white Riesling grape from which its wines are made.

JURA *[Zhu-rah']*
Mountainous region of France near the Swiss border which produces red, white and sparkling wines; Arbois and Château Chalon are probably the best known.

KELLER *[Kell'-er]*
German. "Cellar."

KELLER-ABFÜLLUNG
[Kell'-er-Ahb-fuel'-ung]
German. Estate-bottled. Equivalent to the French *Mis en bouteilles au domaine.* Another term, *Kellerabzug,* has the same meaning. Both indicate that the wine was grown and produced at the particular vineyard specified.

LACHRHYMA CHRISTI
[Lah'-cream ah Krees'-tee]
Wine from the slopes of Vesuvius. Formerly generic term for Italian sparkling wine.

LAFITE-ROTHSCHILD
(CHÂTEAU–) *[Lah-feet' Rote-shield']*
"First Growth" Médoc (Bordeaux), known for great red wines; soft, full-bodied and unbelievable.

LATOUR (CHÂTEAU–) *[Lah-toor']*
"First Growth" Médoc (Bordeaux), also famous for top-ranking Clarets.

MACERATION CARBONIQUE
[Mah-ser-ah'-scion Car-bo-neek']
A process widely used in France whereby fermentation occurs while the juice is still inside the uncrushed grape. The super-grapy "Nouveau" wines made in this way are meant for immediate consumption.

LIVERMORE
A valley in Alameda County renowned for white wines.

MÂCONNAIS *[Mah-kawn'-ay)*
A wine region of Burgundy, south of the Côte d'Or and north of the Beaujolais; the reds are usually sold as "Bourgogne" or "Mâcon."

MADERISÉ *[Mad-air-ee'-zay]*
French. Literally "like Madeira"; term applied to white wine kept past its prime which has turned brown and usually tastes bad.

MAGNUM
A bottle size twice that of the ordinary bottle, or about two-fifths of a gallon. The Jeroboam, a double magnum with a capacity up to 8-1/2 pints, is the largest.

MANZANILLA *[Mahn-tha-nee'-yah]*
Very Sherry-like Spanish wine made in the Sherry country, or just outside.

MARC *[Mar]*
French. Brandy distilled from the leavings of pressed grapes, sometimes from the must.

MARGAUX *[Mar-goe']*
A commune of Médoc in the Bordeaux region, named for a great 'First Growth' château located there.

MARQUE DÉPOSÉE
[Mark dey'-poe-zay']
French. A registered brand name or trademark.

MARSALA *[Mar-sa'-la]*
A sweetish fortified wine from Sicily, first produced for the English market during the Napoleonic period.

MAVRODAPHNE
[Mav'-row-daf'-nee]
A sweet red fortified wine from Greece, often excellent.

MAY WINE
Any light German wine to which the aromatic leaves of the herb *waldmeister* (woodruff) have been added. It is traditionally served cold from a bowl with strawberries floating in it.

MÉDOC *[Meh-dahk']*
The district in the Bordeaux area which is home to most of the officially classified great Clarets. It produces red wines almost exclusively and includes the communes of Pauillac, Margaux, St. Julien, St. Estèphe and St. Laurent.

GLOSSARY

MENDOCINO
The northernmost of California's fine wine counties and one which has begun to increase vineyard acreage most significantly since 1970.

MÉTHODE CHAMPENOISE
[May'-toad shawm-pnwas']
French. Traditional French process for making Champagne.

MEURSAULT *[Mer-so']*
One of the Côte de Beaune communes of Burgundy which produces a top-ranking white wine, dry yet very rich, made entirely from Pinot Chardonnay.

MISE EN BOUTEILLES
AU CHÂTEAU
[Mees'-an-boo-tay'-eh oh-Shah-toe']
French. Literally "château-bottled." *"Mise du Château"* or *"Mise au Domaine"* mean the same thing: that the wine was bottled at the vineyard by the grower. It does not necessarily follow that the wine bottled there was any good.

MONTEREY
Another newly developed California wine county with a great name to come.

MONTRACHET *[Mown-rash-ay']*
Some of the world's greatest white wine is made from Pinot Chardonnay grown in the Burgundy commune Puligny-Montrachet. (Chassagne-Montrachet grows Pinot Blanc.) The best *appellations* are Le Montrachet, Chevalier-Montrachet, Batard-Montrachet, Les Bienvenues and Les Criots.

MOULIN-A-VENT
[Moo'-lan-ah-Vahn]
One of the principal communes of Beaujolais and the name of an outstanding vineyard, home of the very best of Beaujolais, very hearty.

MOUSSEUX *[Moos-soh']*
French. Literally "foaming." Any French sparkling wine other than Champagne made by the *méthode champenoise*.

MOUTON-ROTHSCHILD
(CHÂTEAU–)
[Moo-tohn-Rote-shield']
"Second Growth" Médoc producing red wine of greatness enough to become a *"première cru"* in 1973, the only "1855 classified" château ever promoted.

NAPA
(American Indian word for plenty.) A valley and county north of the San Francisco Bay famous for some of North America's great Cabernet Sauvignon and fine reds and whites generally. The valley is about 35 miles long; its greatest width is about five miles. In addition to "Napa Valley," Napa includes the following localized legal appellations: Carneros, Calistoga, Mt. Veeder, Oakville, Spring Mountain, St. Helena and Yountville.

NATURE *[Nah-tewr']*
French. Unsweetened. Virtually the same meaning as *brut,* denoting the driest sparkling wines.

NEW YORK STATE
The second wine-producing state after California. Its foremost vineyards are concentrated in the Finger Lakes region and around Naples, New York. A full line of New York State wines is made from native American grapes. They have a characteristic "foxy" or "wild-grape" flavor which is often offset by blending with California wines. The sparkling and dry white table wines and rosés are considered the district's best. A small quantity of wine also comes from around Highland in the Hudson River Valley and from Rockland County further south.

NOSE
Scent, odor. "A good nose" means a fine bouquet.

NUITS-ST.-GEORGES
[Nwee-San-Jhorge']
Wine from the commune and principal town of Burgundy's Côte de Nuits (the northern section of the Côte d'Or which produces many of the world's finest red Burgundies). Especially Les St. Georges, Les Porrets, Les Pruliers.

OEIL-DE-PERDRIX
[Oye'-deh-pair-dree]
French. Literally "partridge eye." A traditional term for rosé-looking whites. Called Ramené in Italy.

OLOROSO *[Oh-low-row'-so]*
A sweet Spanish Sherry, full-bodied yet delicate.

ORIGINAL ABFULLÜNG
O-rig'-in-ahl Ahb-fuel'-ung]
German. Literally "Original bottling." This indicates the wine was grown, fermented and bottled at the vineyard by the owners.

ORVIETO *[Or-vee-ay'-toe]*
A fine Italian white wine from the district of Umbria.

PÉTILLANT *[Pet'-ee-ahn]*
French. Slightly sparkling, fizzy. "Crackling."

PIESPORTER *[Pees'-porter]*
Wines grown in the neighborhood of Piesport, some of the very finest Moselles. Piesporter Goldtropfchen is especially famous.

POMACE
Grape skins, pips and sometimes stems left over after pressing out the must. Usually used as fertilizer in the vineyard.

POMMARD *[Poe-mar']*
A Burgundy commune, Côte de Beaune, famous for soft, delicate, smooth red wines.

POUILLY-FUISSÉ
[Poo'-ee Fwee-say']
An excellent white from one of half a dozen villages in the Mâcon area of southern Burgundy. One of the best-value French wines.

POURRITURE NOBLE
[Poo'-ee-tur' Nobl]
French. Literally "noble rot." Same as *edelfaule.*

RESERVA *[Ray-zer'-vah]*
Spanish. "Reserve," specially aged, high quality.

RETSINA *[Rhet-see'-nah]*
Wine with a turpentiny, resinous taste invented by the ancient Greeks. They did not, as is popularly supposed, first start putting pine resin in their wine to keep the Turks from drinking it.

RHEINGAU *[Rhine'-gow]*
A district along the right bank of the Rhine in Germany, eighteen or twenty miles long and only a few miles across at its widest points. From these southward facing vineyards come some of the world's greatest white wines. Rudesheimer, Geisenheimer, Hattenheimer, Schloss Johannisberg, Erbacher, Eltviller and Hochheimer are only a few of the most highly regarded.

RHENISH
English term for Rhine wines in Shakespeare's day, later eclipsed by "hock."

RICHEBOURG *[Reesh'-boor]*
A Burgundy vineyard; part of the Romanée "group" of the Côte de Nuits which produces some of the world's most magnificent red wines.

RIOJA *[Ree-oh'-ha]*
District in the Ebro River Valley of Northern Spain which produces excellent red and white wines. Red Rioja Reservas probably represent the best quality for the money available on the world's wine market today, as long as they aren't being specially promoted by the importer.

ROMANÉE-CONTI
[Row'-mahn-ay'-Kawn'tee]
A celebrated vineyard in Burgundy's Côte de Nuits, adjoining La Romanée and considered to produce the greatest of red Burgundy wines.

SACK
Term for Sherry current in Shakespeare's day (Falstaff was a sack-addict). The origin of the word is variously explained.

SAN BENITO
California winegrowing county just north of Monterey and south of Santa Cruz which includes what is probably the world's largest vineyard.

SANCERRE [Sahn-sair']
A superior white grown in the upper Loire Valley in France and characterized by a beautifully flinty quality. Hemingway's favorite.

SANTA CLARA
A California county south of San Francisco noted for the excellence of its wine, especially that from the Santa Cruz Mountains around Saratoga and Los Gatos.

SANTA CRUZ
A wine-producing county in California which adjoins Santa Clara on the west along the ridge of the Santa Cruz Mountains.

SEKT [Secht]
Any German sparkling wine made by the méthode champenoise.

SOLERA [Sol'-air-ah]
Spanish. A series of casks arranged in tiers for aging and blending Sherry. In a Sherry bodega, the contents of each cask are methodically withdrawn and replenished so that the oldest blends are in the last casks from which the finished Sherry comes.

SONOMA
A leading county in the production of superior California wines, especially reds. It is bounded on the east by Napa County, the Mayacamas Mountains forming the intervening border. Sonoma includes the following appellations; Alexander Valley, Asti, Cloverdale, Healdsburg, Kenwood and Windsor.

SPÄTLESE [Schpayt'-lay-seh]
German. Literally "late selection." Wine made from fully-ripened grapes; often indicates some sweetness.

SPRITZIG [Sprit'-zik]
German. Semi-sparkling, prickly. "Pétillant."

SYBARITE
A refined voluptuary spiritually akin to the inhabitants of the ancient Greek colony of Sybaris, all of whom were legendary wine bibbers. A good word to know.

TAVEL [Tah-vell']
A commune in the Rhône valley not far from Avignon, producing a fairly dry rosé considered among the best in France.

TERROIR [Tehr-wahr']
French. Literally "ground." The special and unique quality with which a given piece of ground imbues a wine is called the "goût du terroir."

TOKAY [Tow-kay']
A celebrated sweet white wine from Tokay, Hungary; California's cheap fortified wine with this name bears no relation to it.

TROCKENBEERENAUSLESE
[Trock'-en-bear'-en-ows'-lay-seh]
German. Literally "individually selected dried berries." Rare, sweet and expensive wine only made in exceptional years, from raisined edelfaule-covered grapes.

VARIETAL
A wine named for the grape from which it is made (providing, under California law, that grape makes up at least 51 percent of the wine). In Europe only Alsatian and Italian wines are known by the names of their grapes.

VERMOUTH
A blended wine which is fortified and infused with aromatic herbs and spices. Vermouths may be dark and sweet or light and dry. Both kinds are generally lighter and drier if made in France rather than in Italy. California also produces some very good vermouths. The name is thought to come from the German word Wermuth, which means wormwood.

VIN DU PAYS [Vahn-due-pay-ee]
French. A term for the local wine of the region, which is rarely marketed outside it.

VITIS LABRUSCA
[Wee'tiss Lah-brus'-kah]
Latin. Species of grapes native to North America, cultivated and hybridized throughout the Eastern United States. "Fox-grapes."

VITIS VINIFERA
[Wee'-tiss Weh-nif-err'-ah]
Latin. Literally "the winebearer vine."
Dominant species of wine grapes
native to Europe, now widely grown
elsewhere as well.

VOLLRADS (SCHLOSS)
[Schlohs Fahl'-rahdz]
One of the greatest Rheingau vineyards producing wines with a magnificent flowery flavor.

VOUGEOT (CLOS DE—)
[Klo-deh-voo-jhoh']
A classic vineyard in the Côte de
Nuits, renowned for its great red Bur-
gundy.

VOUVRAY[Voo'-vray]
A white wine from this region of the
central Loire near Tours; unfailingly
soft, fruity and pleasant. Excellent
sparkling Vouvray is also made.

INDEX

INDEX TO CALIFORNIA WINERIES

BIOGRAPHICAL NOTES

JAMES NORWOOD PRATT

A native North Carolinian, James Norwood Pratt was educated at Chapel Hill and abroad. Since moving to San Francisco in 1965, he has become a leading consumer of California wines and a nationally noted wine author and columnist. Mr. Pratt's recent activities as a film writer, producer and sometime actor have delayed the appearance of his works on women and song, which are still in progress. A classics scholar and a known lover of poetry, he is also husband of the former Charlot Alleta Saunders of Greenwood, Mississippi.

JACQUES de CASO

Early in his career, French-born Jacques de Caso became the first person to catalog the Baron Philippe de Rothschild's art collection (now the *Musée du Vin)* at Chateau Mouton-Rothschild near Bordeaux. Presently a U.S. citizen and a professor of the history of art at the University of California Berkeley, Mr. de Caso is a former Guggenheim Fellow and visiting professor of art at Harvard. He has recently co-authored the monumental *Rodin's Sculpture,* published by the Fine Arts Museums of San Francisco. Messrs. Pratt and de Caso have been collaborating on scholarly and various other projects since they first met in 1970.

SARA RAFFETTO

Sara Raffetto studied art at the University of California at Berkeley and later in Los Angeles with Rico LeBrun. She received a Fulbright in 1961 to study painting in Italy. Her work is represented in numerous private collections. She has illustrated several other 101 books including *Vegetarian Gourmet Cookery* and *The Art of Cooking for Two.*